Individual Studies
for Grade 1

*A Year of Lesson Plans
for Language Arts, Math, and Science*

by
Sonya Shafer

Individual Studies for Grade 1: A Year of Lesson Plans for Language Arts, Math, and Science
© 2016, Sonya Shafer

Cover Design: John Shafer and Sarah Shafer

ISBN 978-1-61634-303-3 printed
ISBN 978-1-61634-304-0 electronic download

Published by
Simply Charlotte Mason, LLC
930 New Hope Road #11-892
Lawrenceville, Georgia 30045
simplycharlottemason.com

Printed by PrintLogic, Inc.
Monroe, Georgia, USA

Contents

How to Use 7
Complete Year's Resources List 8

Term 1 9
    Lesson 1 11
    Lesson 2 11
    Lesson 3 12
    Lesson 4 12
    Lesson 5 13
    Lesson 6 13
    Lesson 7 14
    Lesson 8 14
    Lesson 9 15
    Lesson 10 15
    Lesson 11 16
    Lesson 12 16
    Lesson 13 17
    Lesson 14 17
    Lesson 15 17
    Lesson 16 18
    Lesson 17 18
    Lesson 18 19
    Lesson 19 19
    Lesson 20 20
    Lesson 21 20
    Lesson 22 20
    Lesson 23 21
    Lesson 24 21
    Lesson 25 22
    Lesson 26 22
    Lesson 27 22
    Lesson 28 23
    Lesson 29 23
    Lesson 30 24
    Lesson 31 24
    Lesson 32 25
    Lesson 33 25
    Lesson 34 26
    Lesson 35 26
    Lesson 36 27
    Lesson 37 27
    Lesson 38 28
    Lesson 39 28
    Lesson 40 28
    Lesson 41 29
    Lesson 42 29

Lesson 43 30
Lesson 44 30
Lesson 45 31
Lesson 46 31
Lesson 47 31
Lesson 48 32
Lesson 49 32
Lesson 50 33
Lesson 51 33
Lesson 52 34
Lesson 53 34
Lesson 54 35
Lesson 55 35
Lesson 56 36
Lesson 57 36
Lesson 58 37
Lesson 59 37
Lesson 60 38

Term 2 .... *39*
Lesson 61 41
Lesson 62 41
Lesson 63 42
Lesson 64 42
Lesson 65 42
Lesson 66 43
Lesson 67 43
Lesson 68 44
Lesson 69 44
Lesson 70 45
Lesson 71 45
Lesson 72 45
Lesson 73 46
Lesson 74 46
Lesson 75 47
Lesson 76 47
Lesson 77 48
Lesson 78 48
Lesson 79 48
Lesson 80 49
Lesson 81 49
Lesson 82 50
Lesson 83 50
Lesson 84 51
Lesson 85 51
Lesson 86 51
Lesson 87 52
Lesson 88 52
Lesson 89 53

Lesson 90 53
Lesson 91 54
Lesson 92 54
Lesson 93 55
Lesson 94 55
Lesson 95 56
Lesson 96 56
Lesson 97 57
Lesson 98 57
Lesson 99 58
Lesson 100 58
Lesson 101 59
Lesson 102 59
Lesson 103 59
Lesson 104 60
Lesson 105 60
Lesson 106 61
Lesson 107 61
Lesson 108 62
Lesson 109 62
Lesson 110 63
Lesson 111 63
Lesson 112 64
Lesson 113 64
Lesson 114 64
Lesson 115 65
Lesson 116 65
Lesson 117 66
Lesson 118 66
Lesson 119 67
Lesson 120 67

Term 3 ....*69*
Lesson 121 71
Lesson 122 71
Lesson 123 71
Lesson 124 72
Lesson 125 72
Lesson 126 73
Lesson 127 73
Lesson 128 74
Lesson 129 74
Lesson 130 74
Lesson 131 75
Lesson 132 75
Lesson 133 76
Lesson 134 76
Lesson 135 77
Lesson 136 77

Lesson 137 77
Lesson 138 78
Lesson 139 78
Lesson 140 79
Lesson 141 79
Lesson 142 80
Lesson 143 80
Lesson 144 80
Lesson 145 81
Lesson 146 81
Lesson 147 82
Lesson 148 82
Lesson 149 83
Lesson 150 83
Lesson 151 84
Lesson 152 84
Lesson 153 84
Lesson 154 85
Lesson 155 85
Lesson 156 86
Lesson 157 86
Lesson 158 87
Lesson 159 87
Lesson 160 87
Lesson 161 88
Lesson 162 88
Lesson 163 89
Lesson 164 89
Lesson 165 90
Lesson 166 90
Lesson 167 91
Lesson 168 91
Lesson 169 91
Lesson 170 92
Lesson 171 92
Lesson 172 93
Lesson 173 93
Lesson 174 93
Lesson 175 94
Lesson 176 94
Lesson 177 95
Lesson 178 95
Lesson 179 96
Lesson 180 96

How to Use

Most school subjects can be taught to your whole family together, but some subjects are best taught individually so you can progress at the student's pace. This book of lesson plans contains suggestions and assignments for individual work for students in grade 1. Complete one lesson plan per day to finish these studies in a school year.

The lesson plans in this book cover reading and writing, science, and math.

Reading & Writing

Since students at this young age vary greatly in readiness for reading and writing, we offer two tracks of plans: A and B. Select the track that best fits your student and follow that track's plans throughout the year.

Track A—For students who are just starting out to learn to read and write. They know the letters and the sounds and have done some word building with short vowels, long vowels, and a few blends. They may or may not know how to write the letters.

Track B—For students who can already read many words and short sentences and can print letters but need more practice reading and writing to gain fluency.

Science

Science can be done individually, or if you have more than one student in grades 1–6, they may all do one science course together. Simply Charlotte Mason has several to choose from.

Nature Study is an important part of science studies; be sure to include it. Follow the Nature Study suggestions in your selected science course or use the nature notebook, *Journaling a Year in Nature*, to guide your weekly study. Nature Study can be done all together as a family, but we have included reminders in these individual plans too.

Math

Use the math curriculum of your choice. These lesson plans will include reminders to work on it. As with other individual work, be sure to go at your student's pace.

Complete Year's Resources List

- Math course of choice
- Simply Charlotte Mason science course of choice
- *Journaling a Year in Nature* notebooks, one per person (optional)

Select Track A *or* Track B

Track A

- *Delightful Reading, Level 3: From Words to Books* Kit
- *First Steps*
- *Days Go By*
- *More Days Go By*
- *Delightful Handwriting* teacher book
- *Delightful Handwriting* student copybook

    The *Delightful Handwriting* student copybook is available in two handwriting styles: the traditional print-straight-up-and-down Zaner Bloser and the print-on-a-slant D'Nealian. Select whichever style you prefer. The teacher book contains instructions for both styles.

Track B

- *Busy Times*
- *More Busy Times*
- *A Child's Copybook Reader*, Volumes 1–3

    The copybook readers are available in two handwriting styles: the traditional print-straight-up-and-down Zaner Bloser and the print-on-a-slant D'Nealian. Select whichever style you prefer.

Note: All resources except math are available from Simply Charlotte Mason.

Term 1
(12 weeks; 5 lessons/week)

Term 1 Resources List
- Math course of choice
- Simply Charlotte Mason (SCM) science course of choice
- *Journaling a Year in Nature* notebooks (optional)

Track A
- *Delightful Reading, Level 3: From Words to Books* Kit
- *Delightful Handwriting* teacher book
- *Delightful Handwriting* student copybook
- *First Steps*

Track B
- *A Child's Copybook Reader, Volume 1*
- *Busy Times*

Weekly Schedule *(most weeks)*

	Day One	Day Two	Day Three	Day Four	Day Five
	Math (15–20 min.)	Math (15–20 min.)	Math (15–20 min.)	Math (15–20 min.)	Math (15–20 min.)
		Science (15–20 min.)		Science (15–20 min.)	(Nature Study)
Track A	Delightful Reading (10–15 min.); Delightful Handwriting (5 min.)	Delightful Handwriting (5 min.); First Steps, begins halfway through the term (10–15 min.)	Delightful Reading (10–15 min.)	Delightful Handwriting (5 min.); First Steps, begins halfway through the term (10–15 min.)	Delightful Reading (10–15 min.)
Track B	Copybook Reader (5 min.)	Copybook Reader (5 min.)	Copybook Reader (5 min.); Busy Times (10–15 min.)	Copybook Reader (5 min.)	Busy Times (10–15 min.)

Lesson 1

Materials Needed
- *Delightful Reading, Level 3: From Words to Books* Kit (Track A)
- *A Child's Copybook Reader, Volume 1* (Track B)
- Math course of choice

Tip: Select either Track A or Track B to complete with your student. You need do only one. See page 7 for detailed descriptions.

Track A: Spend 10–15 minutes working on *Delightful Reading, Level 3: From Words to Books*. Go at your student's pace and be sure to stop the lesson before your student loses attention.

Track B: Help your student read aloud *A Child's Copybook Reader, Volume 1*, page 4.

Math: Work on your selected math curriculum for 15–20 minutes.

Lesson 2

Materials Needed
- *Delightful Handwriting* teacher book (Track A)
- *Delightful Handwriting* student copybook (Track A)
- *A Child's Copybook Reader, Volume 1* (Track B)
- Math course of choice
- SCM science course of choice

Track A: Complete Lesson 1 in *Delightful Handwriting*.

Track B: Have your student carefully copy *A Child's Copybook Reader, Volume 1*, page 5. Encourage him to pay close attention as he copies, for when he is done you will ask him how to spell one of the words. When he has finished the copywork, invite him first to spell any word he remembers from the passage. Ask him to spell *and*; if he is unsure, allow him to look at the word.

Tip: Encourage the habits of attention and best effort in copywork lessons by expecting it to be done right the first time. Mistakes or sloppy work requires the student to recopy the entire passage until it is done well.

Math: Work on your selected math curriculum for 15–20 minutes.

Science: In your SCM science course, complete the first assignment for Week 1. Check the suggested schedule in the course book.

Lesson 3

Materials Needed
- *Delightful Reading, Level 3: From Words to Books* Kit (Track A)
- *A Child's Copybook Reader, Volume 1* (Track B)
- Math course of choice

Math: Work on your selected math curriculum for 15–20 minutes.

Track A: Spend 10–15 minutes working on *Delightful Reading, Level 3: From Words to Books.*

Tip: Set the timer for 10 or 15 minutes and when it alerts you, stop the lesson. You can pick up at that point next time.

Track B: Have your student carefully copy *A Child's Copybook Reader, Volume 1,* page 6. Remind him to pay close attention as he copies, for when he is done you will ask him how to spell one of the words. When he has finished the copywork, invite him first to spell any word he remembers. Ask him to spell *all*; if he is unsure, allow him to look at the word.

Tip: You may complete school assignments in any order that works best for your family's schedule. Try to sequence lessons throughout the day to use different parts of the student's brain and body as you go along. In other words, don't schedule two "book-heavy" assignments back to back. Put the math assignment in between or do some Family work—such as Picture Study or Music Study—in between to break up the readings. Each lesson plan in this book is sequenced to help you with that important principle.

Lesson 4

Materials Needed
- *Delightful Handwriting* teacher book (Track A)
- *Delightful Handwriting* student copybook (Track A)
- *A Child's Copybook Reader, Volume 1* (Track B)
- Math course of choice
- SCM science course of choice

Track A: Complete Lesson 2 in *Delightful Handwriting.*

Track B: Have your student carefully copy *A Child's Copybook Reader, Volume 1,* page 7. When he has finished the copywork, invite him to spell any word he remembers. Ask him to spell *things*; if he is unsure, allow him to look at the word.

Math: Work on your selected math curriculum for 15–20 minutes.

Tip: If you are not able to complete the math lesson in 15–20 minutes, you can schedule another 15- or 20-minute time slot later in the day to finish (if you think it is necessary to do so).

Science: In your SCM science course, complete the second assignment for Week 1.

Lesson 5

Materials Needed
- *Delightful Reading, Level 3: From Words to Books* Kit (Track A)
- *Busy Times* (Track B)
- Math course of choice
- (Optional) *Journaling a Year in Nature* notebooks

Math: Work on your selected math curriculum for 15–20 minutes.

Track A: Spend 10–15 minutes working on *Delightful Reading, Level 3: From Words to Books.*

Track B: Help your student read aloud *Busy Times*, pages 6–16, "A Warm Day."

Tip: Don't worry if your student doesn't get through all of pages 6–16. There is a scheduled catch-up time in lesson 8.

Nature Study: Take the whole family outside for nature study.

Tip: Follow the Nature Study suggestions in your SCM science course or use the nature notebooks, Journaling a Year in Nature, *to guide your weekly nature study.*

Lesson 6

Materials Needed
- *Delightful Reading, Level 3: From Words to Books* Kit (Track A)
- *A Child's Copybook Reader, Volume 1* (Track B)
- Math course of choice

Track A: Spend 10–15 minutes working on *Delightful Reading, Level 3: From Words to Books.*

Track B: Have your student carefully copy *A Child's Copybook Reader, Volume*

Notes

1, page 8. When he has finished the copywork, invite him to spell any word he remembers. Ask him to spell *them*; if he is unsure, allow him to look at the word.

Tip: Feel free to jot down his selected words over in the Notes column so you can easily refer to them for periodic reviews.

Math: Work on your selected math curriculum for 15–20 minutes.

Lesson 7

Materials Needed
- *Delightful Handwriting* teacher book (Track A)
- *Delightful Handwriting* student copybook (Track A)
- *A Child's Copybook Reader, Volume 1* (Track B)
- Math course of choice
- SCM science course of choice

Track A: Complete Lesson 3 in *Delightful Handwriting*.

Track B: Help your student read aloud *A Child's Copybook Reader, Volume 1*, page 9.

Math: Work on your selected math curriculum for 15–20 minutes.

Science: In your SCM science course, complete the first assignment for Week 2.

Tip: Oral narration lays the foundation for solid composition skills. Make sure your student is giving several oral narrations each week from his history, science, geography, or Bible readings. (Download the free e-book, Five Steps to Successful Narration, *at simplycm.com/fivesteps for helpful how-to's.)*

Lesson 8

Materials Needed
- *Delightful Reading, Level 3: From Words to Books* Kit (Track A)
- *A Child's Copybook Reader, Volume 1* (Track B)
- *Busy Times*, if needed (Track B)
- Math course of choice

Math: Work on your selected math curriculum for 15–20 minutes.

Track A: Spend 10–15 minutes working on *Delightful Reading, Level 3: From Words to Books*.

Track B: Have your student carefully copy *A Child's Copybook Reader, Volume 1*, page 10. When he has finished the copywork, invite him to spell any word he remembers. Ask him to spell *each*; if he is unsure, allow him to look at the word.

Help your student finish reading aloud *Busy Times*, pages 6–16, "A Warm Day," if needed.

Lesson 9

Materials Needed
- *Delightful Handwriting* teacher book (Track A)
- *Delightful Handwriting* student copybook (Track A)
- *A Child's Copybook Reader, Volume 1* (Track B)
- Math course of choice
- SCM science course of choice

Track A: Complete Lesson 4 in *Delightful Handwriting*.

Track B: Have your student carefully copy *A Child's Copybook Reader, Volume 1*, page 11. When he has finished the copywork, invite him to spell any word he remembers. Ask him to spell *that*; if he is unsure, allow him to look at the word.

Math: Work on your selected math curriculum for 15–20 minutes.

Science: In your SCM science course, complete the second assignment for Week 2.

Lesson 10

Materials Needed
- *Delightful Reading, Level 3: From Words to Books* Kit (Track A)
- *Busy Times* (Track B)
- Math course of choice
- (Optional) *Journaling a Year in Nature* notebooks

Math: Work on your selected math curriculum for 15–20 minutes.

Track A: Spend 10–15 minutes working on *Delightful Reading, Level 3: From Words to Books*.

Track B: Help your student read aloud *Busy Times*, pages 17–24, "A Good Dog."

Tip: Don't worry if your student doesn't get through all of pages 17–24. There is a scheduled catch-up time in lesson 12.

Nature Study: Take the whole family outside for nature study.

Notes

Tip: Follow the Nature Study suggestions in your SCM science course or use the nature notebooks, Journaling a Year in Nature, *to guide your weekly nature study.*

Lesson 11

Materials Needed
- *Delightful Reading, Level 3: From Words to Books* Kit (Track A)
- *A Child's Copybook Reader, Volume 1* (Track B)
- Math course of choice

Track A: Spend 10–15 minutes working on *Delightful Reading, Level 3: From Words to Books.*

Track B: Have your student carefully copy *A Child's Copybook Reader, Volume 1,* page 12. When he has finished the copywork, invite him to spell any word he remembers. Ask him to spell *made*; if he is unsure, allow him to look at the word.

Math: Work on your selected math curriculum for 15–20 minutes.

Lesson 12

Materials Needed
- *Delightful Handwriting* teacher book (Track A)
- *Delightful Handwriting* student copybook (Track A)
- *A Child's Copybook Reader, Volume 1* (Track B)
- *Busy Times*, if needed (Track B)
- Math course of choice
- SCM science course of choice

Track A: Complete Lesson 5 in *Delightful Handwriting.*

Track B: Help your student finish reading aloud *Busy Times*, pages 17–24, "A Good Dog," if needed.

Have your student carefully copy *A Child's Copybook Reader, Volume 1,* page 13. When he has finished the copywork, invite him to spell any word he remembers. Ask him to spell *their*; if he is unsure, allow him to look at the word.

Tip: Many of the words that you are asking for in these gentle spelling exercises are from the 100 Most Commonly Used words your student learned in Delightful Reading, *Levels 2 and 3.*

Math: Work on your selected math curriculum for 15–20 minutes.

Science: In your SCM science course, complete the first assignment for Week 3.

Lesson 13

Materials Needed
- *Delightful Reading, Level 3: From Words to Books* Kit (Track A)
- *A Child's Copybook Reader, Volume 1* (Track B)
- Math course of choice

Math: Work on your selected math curriculum for 15–20 minutes.

Track A: Spend 10–15 minutes working on *Delightful Reading, Level 3: From Words to Books.*

Track B: Help your student read aloud *A Child's Copybook Reader, Volume 1,* page 14.

Lesson 14

Materials Needed
- *Delightful Handwriting* teacher book (Track A)
- *Delightful Handwriting* student copybook (Track A)
- *A Child's Copybook Reader, Volume 1* (Track B)
- Math course of choice
- SCM science course of choice

Track A: Complete Lesson 6 in *Delightful Handwriting.*

Track B: Have your student carefully copy *A Child's Copybook Reader, Volume 1,* page 15. When he has finished the copywork, invite him to spell any word he remembers. Ask him to spell *in*; if he is unsure, allow him to look at the word.

Math: Work on your selected math curriculum for 15–20 minutes.

Science: In your SCM science course, complete the second assignment for Week 3.

Lesson 15

Materials Needed
- *Delightful Reading, Level 3: From Words to Books* Kit (Track A)
- *Busy Times* (Track B)
- Math course of choice
- (Optional) *Journaling a Year in Nature* notebooks

Math: Work on your selected math curriculum for 15–20 minutes.

Track A: Spend 10–15 minutes working on *Delightful Reading, Level 3: From Words to Books.*

Track B: Help your student read aloud *Busy Times*, pages 25–34, "Rover and the Wagon."

Tip: Don't worry if your student doesn't get through all of pages 25–34. There is a scheduled catch-up time in lesson 17. You can also take turns reading one page each as you and your student work your way through the chapter.

Nature Study: Take the whole family outside for nature study.

Tip: Follow the Nature Study suggestions in your SCM science course or use the nature notebooks, Journaling a Year in Nature, *to guide your weekly nature study.*

Lesson 16

Materials Needed
- *Delightful Reading, Level 3: From Words to Books* Kit (Track A)
- *A Child's Copybook Reader, Volume 1* (Track B)
- Math course of choice

Track A: Spend 10–15 minutes working on *Delightful Reading, Level 3: From Words to Books*.

Track B: Have your student carefully copy *A Child's Copybook Reader, Volume 1*, page 16. When he has finished the copywork, invite him to spell any word he remembers. Ask him to spell *at*; if he is unsure, allow him to look at the word.

Math: Work on your selected math curriculum for 15–20 minutes.

Lesson 17

Materials Needed
- *Delightful Handwriting* teacher book (Track A)
- *Delightful Handwriting* student copybook (Track A)
- *A Child's Copybook Reader, Volume 1* (Track B)
- *Busy Times*, if needed (Track B)
- Math course of choice
- SCM science course of choice

Track A: Complete Lesson 7 in *Delightful Handwriting*.

Track B: Have your student carefully copy *A Child's Copybook Reader, Volume 1*, page 17. When he has finished the copywork, invite him to spell any word he remembers. Ask him to spell *God*; if he is unsure, allow him to look at the word.

Help your student finish reading aloud *Busy Times*, pages 25–34, "Rover and the Wagon," if needed.

Math: Work on your selected math curriculum for 15–20 minutes.

Science: In your SCM science course, complete the first assignment for Week 4.

Reminder: Get First Steps *for Track A for lesson 27.*

Lesson 18

Materials Needed
- *Delightful Reading, Level 3: From Words to Books* Kit (Track A)
- *A Child's Copybook Reader, Volume 1* (Track B)
- Math course of choice

Math: Work on your selected math curriculum for 15–20 minutes.

Track A: Spend 10–15 minutes working on *Delightful Reading, Level 3: From Words to Books*.

Track B: Have your student carefully copy *A Child's Copybook Reader, Volume 1*, page 18. When he has finished the copywork, invite him to spell any word he remembers. If desired, review 6–10 of these words and his selected words from previous copywork lessons: *and, all, things, them, each, that, made, their, in, at, God*. If your student is unsure about a particular word's spelling, allow him to look at the word.

Tip: Don't encourage guessing during these lessons; you want him to see the word spelled correctly as much as possible.

Lesson 19

Materials Needed
- *Delightful Handwriting* teacher book (Track A)
- *Delightful Handwriting* student copybook (Track A)
- *A Child's Copybook Reader, Volume 1* (Track B)
- Math course of choice
- SCM science course of choice

Track A: Complete Lesson 8 in *Delightful Handwriting*.

Track B: Help your student read aloud *A Child's Copybook Reader, Volume 1*, page 19.

Math: Work on your selected math curriculum for 15–20 minutes.

Science: In your SCM science course, complete the second assignment for Week 4.

Lesson 20

Materials Needed
- *Delightful Reading, Level 3: From Words to Books* Kit (Track A)
- *Busy Times* (Track B)
- Math course of choice
- (Optional) *Journaling a Year in Nature* notebooks

Math: Work on your selected math curriculum for 15–20 minutes.

Track A: Spend 10–15 minutes working on *Delightful Reading, Level 3: From Words to Books*.

Track B: Help your student read aloud *Busy Times*, pages 36–43, "A Pet Goat."

Tip: Don't worry if your student doesn't get through all of pages 36–43. There is a scheduled catch-up time in lesson 22.

Nature Study: Take the whole family outside for nature study.

Lesson 21

Materials Needed
- *Delightful Reading, Level 3: From Words to Books* Kit (Track A)
- *A Child's Copybook Reader, Volume 1* (Track B)
- Math course of choice

Track A: Spend 10–15 minutes working on *Delightful Reading, Level 3: From Words to Books*.

Track B: Have your student carefully copy *A Child's Copybook Reader, Volume 1*, page 20. When he has finished the copywork, invite him to spell any word he remembers. Ask him to spell *the*; if he is unsure, allow him to look at the word.

Math: Work on your selected math curriculum for 15–20 minutes.

Lesson 22

Materials Needed
- *Delightful Handwriting* teacher book (Track A)
- *Delightful Handwriting* student copybook (Track A)
- *A Child's Copybook Reader, Volume 1* (Track B)

- *Busy Times*, if needed (Track B)
- Math course of choice
- SCM science course of choice

Track A: Complete Lesson 9 in *Delightful Handwriting*.

Track B: Help your student finish reading aloud *Busy Times*, pages 36–43, "A Pet Goat," if needed.

Have your student carefully copy *A Child's Copybook Reader, Volume 1*, page 21. When he has finished the copywork, invite him to spell any word he remembers. Ask him to spell *run* and to look closely and tell how the word changes when *ing* is added to the end. Ask him to spell *running*; if he is unsure, allow him to look at the word.

Math: Work on your selected math curriculum for 15–20 minutes.

Science: In your SCM science course, complete the first assignment for Week 5.

Lesson 23

Materials Needed
- *Delightful Reading, Level 3: From Words to Books* Kit (Track A)
- *A Child's Copybook Reader, Volume 1* (Track B)
- Math course of choice

Math: Work on your selected math curriculum for 15–20 minutes.

Track A: Spend 10–15 minutes working on *Delightful Reading, Level 3: From Words to Books*.

Track B: Have your student carefully copy *A Child's Copybook Reader, Volume 1*, page 22. When he has finished the copywork, invite him to spell any word he remembers. Ask him to spell *sunset*. Encourage him to think of the two shorter words that are put together to form *sunset*; if he is unsure, allow him to look at the word.

Lesson 24

Materials Needed
- *Delightful Handwriting* teacher book (Track A)
- *Delightful Handwriting* student copybook (Track A)
- *A Child's Copybook Reader, Volume 1* (Track B)
- Math course of choice
- SCM science course of choice

Track A: Complete Lesson 10 in *Delightful Handwriting*.

Track B: Have your student carefully copy *A Child's Copybook Reader, Volume 1*, page 23. When he has finished the copywork, invite him to spell any word he remembers. Ask him to spell *up*; if he is unsure, allow him to look at the word.

Math: Work on your selected math curriculum for 15–20 minutes.

Science: In your SCM science course, complete the second assignment for Week 5.

Lesson 25

Materials Needed
- *Delightful Reading, Level 3: From Words to Books* Kit (Track A)
- *Busy Times* (Track B)
- Math course of choice
- (Optional) *Journaling a Year in Nature* notebooks

Math: Work on your selected math curriculum for 15–20 minutes.

Track A: Spend 10–15 minutes working on *Delightful Reading, Level 3: From Words to Books*.

Track B: Help your student read aloud *Busy Times*, pages 44–52, "The Goat Cart."

Tip: Don't worry if your student doesn't get through all of pages 44–52. There is a scheduled catch-up time in lesson 27.

Nature Study: Take the whole family outside for nature study.

Lesson 26

Materials Needed
- *Delightful Reading, Level 3: From Words to Books* Kit (Track A)
- *A Child's Copybook Reader, Volume 1* (Track B)
- Math course of choice

Track A: Spend 10–15 minutes working on *Delightful Reading, Level 3: From Words to Books*.

Track B: Help your student read aloud *A Child's Copybook Reader, Volume 1*, page 24.

Math: Work on your selected math curriculum for 15–20 minutes.

Lesson 27

Materials Needed
- *Delightful Handwriting* teacher book (Track A)

- *Delightful Handwriting* student copybook (Track A)
- *First Steps* (Track A)
- *A Child's Copybook Reader, Volume 1* (Track B)
- *Busy Times*, if needed (Track B)
- Math course of choice
- SCM science course of choice

Track A: Complete Lesson 11 in *Delightful Handwriting*.

Help your student read aloud *First Steps*, pages 5–11, "The New Horse." You will read the first part of the story, then your student will finish it.

_____

Tip: Don't worry if your student doesn't get all the way through pages 5–11. You will have time to catch up in lesson 29.
_____

Track B: Have your student carefully copy *A Child's Copybook Reader, Volume 1*, page 25. When he has finished the copywork, invite him to spell any word he remembers. Ask him to spell *winter*; if he is unsure, allow him to look at the word.

Help your student finish reading aloud *Busy Times*, pages 44–52, "The Goat Cart," if needed.

Math: Work on your selected math curriculum for 15–20 minutes.

Science: In your SCM science course, complete the first assignment for Week 6.

Lesson 28

Materials Needed
- *Delightful Reading, Level 3: From Words to Books* Kit (Track A)
- *A Child's Copybook Reader, Volume 1* (Track B)
- Math course of choice

Math: Work on your selected math curriculum for 15–20 minutes.

Track A: Spend 10–15 minutes working on *Delightful Reading, Level 3: From Words to Books*.

Track B: Have your student carefully copy *A Child's Copybook Reader, Volume 1*, page 26. When he has finished the copywork, invite him to spell any word he remembers. Ask him to spell *summer*; if he is unsure, allow him to look at the word.

Lesson 29

Materials Needed
- *Delightful Handwriting* teacher book (Track A)
- *Delightful Handwriting* student copybook (Track A)

- *First Steps*, if needed (Track A)
- *A Child's Copybook Reader, Volume 1* (Track B)
- Math course of choice
- SCM science course of choice

Track A: Complete Lesson 12 in *Delightful Handwriting*.

Help your student finish reading aloud *First Steps*, pages 5–11, "The New Horse," if needed.

Track B: Have your student carefully copy *A Child's Copybook Reader, Volume 1*, page 27. When he has finished the copywork, invite him to spell any word he remembers. Ask him to spell *garden*; if he is unsure, allow him to look at the word.

Math: Work on your selected math curriculum for 15–20 minutes.

Science: In your SCM science course, complete the second assignment for Week 6.

Lesson 30

Materials Needed
- *Delightful Reading, Level 3: From Words to Books* Kit (Track A)
- *Busy Times* (Track B)
- Math course of choice
- (Optional) *Journaling a Year in Nature* notebooks

Math: Work on your selected math curriculum for 15–20 minutes.

Track A: Spend 10–15 minutes working on *Delightful Reading, Level 3: From Words to Books*.

Track B: Help your student read aloud *Busy Times*, pages 53–61, "Whiskers and the Cart."

Tip: Don't worry if your student doesn't get through all of pages 53–61. There is a scheduled catch-up time in lesson 33.

Nature Study: Take the whole family outside for nature study.

Lesson 31

Materials Needed
- *Delightful Reading, Level 3: From Words to Books* Kit (Track A)
- *Delightful Handwriting* teacher book (Track A)
- *Delightful Handwriting* student copybook (Track A)
- *A Child's Copybook Reader, Volume 1* (Track B)
- Math course of choice

Track A: Spend 10–15 minutes working on *Delightful Reading, Level 3: From Words to Books.*

Complete Lesson 13 in *Delightful Handwriting.*

Track B: Have your student carefully copy A *Child's Copybook Reader, Volume 1,* page 28. When he has finished the copywork, invite him to spell any word he remembers. Ask him to spell *one;* if he is unsure, allow him to look at the word.

Math: Work on your selected math curriculum for 15–20 minutes.

Lesson 32

Materials Needed
- *Delightful Handwriting* teacher book (Track A)
- *Delightful Handwriting* student copybook (Track A)
- *First Steps* (Track A)
- *A Child's Copybook Reader, Volume 1* (Track B)
- Math course of choice
- SCM science course of choice

Track A: Complete Lesson 14 in *Delightful Handwriting.*

Help your student read aloud *First Steps*, pages 12–17, "The Little Wagon." You will read the first part of the story, then your student will finish it.

Tip: Don't worry if your student doesn't get all the way through pages 12–17. You will have time to catch up in lesson 34.

Track B: Help your student read aloud *A Child's Copybook Reader, Volume 1,* page 29.

Math: Work on your selected math curriculum for 15–20 minutes.

Science: In your SCM science course, complete the first assignment for Week 7.

Lesson 33

Materials Needed
- *Delightful Reading, Level 3: From Words to Books* Kit (Track A)
- *A Child's Copybook Reader, Volume 1* (Track B)
- *Busy Times*, if needed (Track B)
- Math course of choice

Math: Work on your selected math curriculum for 15–20 minutes.

Track A: Spend 10–15 minutes working on *Delightful Reading, Level 3: From Words to Books.*

Track B: Help your student finish reading aloud *Busy Times*, pages 53–61, "Whiskers and the Cart," if needed.

Have your student carefully copy *A Child's Copybook Reader, Volume 1*, page 30. When he has finished the copywork, invite him to spell any word he remembers. Ask him to spell *trees*; if he is unsure, allow him to look at the word.

Lesson 34

Materials Needed
- *Delightful Handwriting* teacher book (Track A)
- *Delightful Handwriting* student copybook (Track A)
- *First Steps*, if needed (Track A)
- *A Child's Copybook Reader, Volume 1* (Track B)
- Math course of choice
- SCM science course of choice

Track A: Complete Lesson 15 in *Delightful Handwriting*.

Help your student finish reading aloud *First Steps*, pages 12–17, "The Little Wagon," if needed.

Track B: Have your student carefully copy *A Child's Copybook Reader, Volume 1*, page 31. When he has finished the copywork, invite him to spell any word he remembers. Ask him to spell *we*; if he is unsure, allow him to look at the word.

Math: Work on your selected math curriculum for 15–20 minutes.

Science: In your SCM science course, complete the second assignment for Week 7.

Lesson 35

Materials Needed
- *Delightful Reading, Level 3: From Words to Books* Kit (Track A)
- *Busy Times* (Track B)
- Math course of choice
- (Optional) *Journaling a Year in Nature* notebooks

Math: Work on your selected math curriculum for 15–20 minutes.

Track A: Spend 10–15 minutes working on *Delightful Reading, Level 3: From Words to Books*.

Track B: Help your student read aloud *Busy Times*, pages 62–72, "Peter Forgets."

Tip: Don't worry if your student doesn't get through all of pages 62–72. There is a scheduled catch-up time in lesson 37.

Nature Study: Take the whole family outside for nature study.

Lesson 36

Materials Needed
- *Delightful Reading, Level 3: From Words to Books* Kit (Track A)
- *Delightful Handwriting* teacher book (Track A)
- *Delightful Handwriting* student copybook (Track A)
- *A Child's Copybook Reader, Volume 1* (Track B)
- Math course of choice

Track A: Spend 10–15 minutes working on *Delightful Reading, Level 3: From Words to Books*.
Complete Lesson 16 in *Delightful Handwriting*.

Track B: Have your student carefully copy *A Child's Copybook Reader, Volume 1*, page 32. When he has finished the copywork, invite him to spell any word he remembers. Ask him to spell *water*; if he is unsure, allow him to look at the word.

Math: Work on your selected math curriculum for 15–20 minutes.

Lesson 37

Materials Needed
- *Delightful Handwriting* teacher book (Track A)
- *Delightful Handwriting* student copybook (Track A)
- *First Steps* (Track A)
- *A Child's Copybook Reader, Volume 1* (Track B)
- *Busy Times*, if needed (Track B)
- Math course of choice
- SCM science course of choice

Track A: Complete Lesson 17 in *Delightful Handwriting*.
Help your student read aloud *First Steps*, pages 18–25, "Rides, Rides, Rides." You will read the first part of the story, then your student will finish it.

Tip: Don't worry if your student doesn't get all the way through pages 18–25. You will have time to catch up in lesson 39.

Track B: Have your student carefully copy *A Child's Copybook Reader, Volume 1*, page 33. When he has finished the copywork, invite him to spell any word he remembers. Ask him to spell *day*; if he is unsure, allow him to look at the word.
Help your student finish reading aloud *Busy Times*, pages 62–72, "Peter Forgets," if needed.

Math: Work on your selected math curriculum for 15–20 minutes.

Science: In your SCM science course, complete the first assignment for Week 8.

Lesson 38

Materials Needed
- *Delightful Reading, Level 3: From Words to Books* Kit (Track A)
- *A Child's Copybook Reader, Volume 1* (Track B)
- Math course of choice

Math: Work on your selected math curriculum for 15–20 minutes.

Track A: Spend 10–15 minutes working on *Delightful Reading, Level 3: From Words to Books*.

Track B: Help your student read aloud *A Child's Copybook Reader, Volume 1*, page 34.

Lesson 39

Materials Needed
- *Delightful Handwriting* teacher book (Track A)
- *Delightful Handwriting* student copybook (Track A)
- *First Steps*, if needed (Track A)
- *A Child's Copybook Reader, Volume 1* (Track B)
- Math course of choice
- SCM science course of choice

Track A: Complete Lesson 18 in *Delightful Handwriting*.

Help your student finish reading aloud *First Steps*, pages 18–25, "Rides, Rides, Rides," if needed.

Track B: Have your student carefully copy *A Child's Copybook Reader, Volume 1*, page 35. When he has finished the copywork, invite him to spell any word he remembers. Ask him to spell *see*; if he is unsure, allow him to look at the word.

Math: Work on your selected math curriculum for 15–20 minutes.

Science: In your SCM science course, complete the second assignment for Week 8.

Lesson 40

Materials Needed
- *Delightful Reading, Level 3: From Words to Books* Kit (Track A)
- *Busy Times* (Track B)
- Math course of choice
- (Optional) *Journaling a Year in Nature* notebooks

Math: Work on your selected math curriculum for 15–20 minutes.

Track A: Spend 10–15 minutes working on *Delightful Reading, Level 3: From Words to Books.*

Track B: Help your student read aloud *Busy Times*, pages 73–82, "Good-by, Goat Cart."

Tip: Don't worry if your student doesn't get through all of pages 73–82. There is a scheduled catch-up time in lesson 42.

Nature Study: Take the whole family outside for nature study.

Lesson 41

Materials Needed
- *Delightful Reading, Level 3: From Words to Books* Kit (Track A)
- *Delightful Handwriting* teacher book (Track A)
- *Delightful Handwriting* student copybook (Track A)
- *A Child's Copybook Reader, Volume 1* (Track B)
- Math course of choice

Track A: Spend 10–15 minutes working on *Delightful Reading, Level 3: From Words to Books.*
Complete Lesson 19 in *Delightful Handwriting.*

Track B: Have your student carefully copy *A Child's Copybook Reader, Volume 1*, page 36. When he has finished the copywork, invite him to spell any word he remembers. Ask him to spell *tell*; if he is unsure, allow him to look at the word.

Math: Work on your selected math curriculum for 15–20 minutes.

Lesson 42

Materials Needed
- *Delightful Handwriting* teacher book (Track A)
- *Delightful Handwriting* student copybook (Track A)
- *First Steps* (Track A)
- *A Child's Copybook Reader, Volume 1* (Track B)
- *Busy Times*, if needed (Track B)
- Math course of choice
- SCM science course of choice

Track A: Complete Lesson 20 in *Delightful Handwriting.*
Help your student read aloud *First Steps*, pages 26–30, "Ride with Me."

Tip: Don't worry if your student doesn't get all the way through pages 26–30. You will have time to catch up in lesson 44.

Track B: Help your student finish reading aloud *Busy Times*, pages 73–82, "Good-by, Goat Cart," if needed.

Have your student carefully copy *A Child's Copybook Reader, Volume 1*, page 37. When he has finished the copywork, invite him to spell any word he remembers. Ask him to spell *is*; if he is unsure, allow him to look at the word.

Math: Work on your selected math curriculum for 15–20 minutes.

Science: In your SCM science course, complete the first assignment for Week 9.

Lesson 43

Materials Needed
- *Delightful Reading, Level 3: From Words to Books* Kit (Track A)
- *A Child's Copybook Reader, Volume 1* (Track B)
- Math course of choice

Math: Work on your selected math curriculum for 15–20 minutes.

Track A: Spend 10–15 minutes working on *Delightful Reading, Level 3: From Words to Books.*

Track B: Have your student carefully copy *A Child's Copybook Reader, Volume 1*, page 38. When he has finished the copywork, invite him to spell any word he remembers. Ask him to spell *has*; if he is unsure, allow him to look at the word. See if he can also spell *had*.

Lesson 44

Materials Needed
- *Delightful Handwriting* teacher book (Track A)
- *Delightful Handwriting* student copybook (Track A)
- *First Steps*, if needed (Track A)
- *A Child's Copybook Reader, Volume 1* (Track B)
- Math course of choice
- SCM science course of choice

Track A: Complete Lesson 21 in *Delightful Handwriting.*

Help your student finish reading aloud *First Steps*, pages 26–30, "Ride with Me," if needed.

Track B: Help your student read aloud the entire poem, "All Things Bright and Beautiful," in *A Child's Copybook Reader, Volume 1*, page 39. If desired, review 6–10 of these words and his selected words from previous copywork lessons: *the, running, sunset, up, winter, summer, garden, one, trees, we, water, day, see, tell, is, has, had.* If your student is unsure about a particular word's spelling, allow him to look at the word.

Math: Work on your selected math curriculum for 15–20 minutes.

Science: In your SCM science course, complete the second assignment for Week 9.

Lesson 45

Materials Needed
- *Delightful Reading, Level 3: From Words to Books* Kit (Track A)
- *Busy Times* (Track B)
- Math course of choice
- (Optional) *Journaling a Year in Nature* notebooks

Math: Work on your selected math curriculum for 15–20 minutes.

Track A: Spend 10–15 minutes working on *Delightful Reading, Level 3: From Words to Books*.

Track B: Help your student read aloud *Busy Times*, pages 84–92, "New Work for Peter."

Tip: Don't worry if your student doesn't get through all of pages 84–92. There is a scheduled catch-up time in lesson 47.

Nature Study: Take the whole family outside for nature study.

Lesson 46

Materials Needed
- *Delightful Reading, Level 3: From Words to Books* Kit (Track A)
- *Delightful Handwriting* teacher book (Track A)
- *Delightful Handwriting* student copybook (Track A)
- *A Child's Copybook Reader, Volume 1* (Track B)
- Math course of choice

Track A: Spend 10–15 minutes working on *Delightful Reading, Level 3: From Words to Books*.
   Complete Lesson 22 in *Delightful Handwriting*.

Track B: Help your student read aloud *A Child's Copybook Reader, Volume 1*, page 41.

Math: Work on your selected math curriculum for 15–20 minutes.

Lesson 47

Materials Needed
- *Delightful Handwriting* teacher book (Track A)

Notes

- *Delightful Handwriting* student copybook (Track A)
- *First Steps* (Track A)
- *A Child's Copybook Reader, Volume 1* (Track B)
- *Busy Times*, if needed (Track B)
- Math course of choice
- SCM science course of choice

Track A: Complete Lesson 23 in *Delightful Handwriting*.

Help your student read aloud *First Steps*, pages 31–37, "Miriam." You will read the first part of the story, then your student will finish it.

_____

Tip: Don't worry if your student doesn't get all the way through pages 31–37. You will have time to catch up in lesson 49.

_____

Track B: Have your student carefully copy the first sentence of the fable in *A Child's Copybook Reader, Volume 1*, page 42: "Two frogs lived together in a marsh." When he has finished the copywork, invite him to spell any word he remembers. Ask him to spell *two*; if he is unsure, allow him to look at the word.

Help your student finish reading aloud *Busy Times*, pages 84–92, "New Work for Peter," if needed.

Math: Work on your selected math curriculum for 15–20 minutes.

Science: In your SCM science course, complete the first assignment for Week 10.

Lesson 48

Materials Needed
- *Delightful Reading, Level 3: From Words to Books* Kit (Track A)
- *A Child's Copybook Reader, Volume 1* (Track B)
- Math course of choice

Math: Work on your selected math curriculum for 15–20 minutes.

Track A: Spend 10–15 minutes working on *Delightful Reading, Level 3: From Words to Books*.

Track B: Have your student carefully copy the next phrase of the fable in *A Child's Copybook Reader, Volume 1*, beginning on page 43: "But one hot summer the marsh dried up,". When he has finished the copywork, invite him to spell any word he remembers. Ask him to spell *but*; if he is unsure, allow him to look at the word.

Lesson 49

Materials Needed
- *Delightful Handwriting* teacher book (Track A)

- *Delightful Handwriting* student copybook (Track A)
- *First Steps*, if needed (Track A)
- *A Child's Copybook Reader, Volume 1* (Track B)
- Math course of choice
- SCM science course of choice

Track A: Complete Lesson 24 in *Delightful Handwriting*.

Help your student finish reading aloud *First Steps*, pages 31–37, "Miriam," if needed.

Track B: Have your student carefully copy the next phrase of the fable in *A Child's Copybook Reader, Volume 1*, beginning on page 44: "and they left it to look for another place to live in,". When he has finished the copywork, invite him to spell any word he remembers. Ask him to spell *look*; if he is unsure, allow him to look at the word.

Math: Work on your selected math curriculum for 15–20 minutes.

Science: In your SCM science course, complete the second assignment for Week 10.

Lesson 50

Materials Needed
- *Delightful Reading, Level 3: From Words to Books* Kit (Track A)
- *Busy Times* (Track B)
- Math course of choice
- (Optional) *Journaling a Year in Nature* notebooks

Math: Work on your selected math curriculum for 15–20 minutes.

Track A: Spend 10–15 minutes working on *Delightful Reading, Level 3: From Words to Books*.

Track B: Help your student read aloud *Busy Times*, pages 93–98, "The Golden Rule."

Tip: Don't worry if your student doesn't get through all of pages 93–98. There is a scheduled catch-up time in lesson 53.

Nature Study: Take the whole family outside for nature study.

Lesson 51

Materials Needed
- *Delightful Reading, Level 3: From Words to Books* Kit (Track A)
- *Delightful Handwriting* teacher book (Track A)

Notes

- *Delightful Handwriting* student copybook (Track A)
- *A Child's Copybook Reader, Volume 1* (Track B)
- Math course of choice

Track A: Spend 10–15 minutes working on *Delightful Reading, Level 3: From Words to Books*.
Complete Lesson 25 in *Delightful Handwriting*.

Track B: Have your student carefully copy the rest of the sentence in *A Child's Copybook Reader, Volume 1*, beginning on page 45: "for frogs like damp places if they can get them." When he has finished the copywork, invite him to spell any word he remembers. Ask him to spell *get*; if he is unsure, allow him to look at the word.

Math: Work on your selected math curriculum for 15–20 minutes.

Lesson 52

Materials Needed
- *Delightful Handwriting* teacher book (Track A)
- *Delightful Handwriting* student copybook (Track A)
- *First Steps* (Track A)
- *A Child's Copybook Reader, Volume 1* (Track B)
- Math course of choice
- SCM science course of choice

Track A: Complete Lesson 26 in *Delightful Handwriting*.
Help your student read aloud *First Steps*, pages 38–46, "I See Something."

Tip: Don't worry if your student doesn't get all the way through pages 38–46. You will have time to catch up in lesson 54.

Track B: Help your student read aloud *A Child's Copybook Reader, Volume 1*, page 47.

Math: Work on your selected math curriculum for 15–20 minutes.

Science: In your SCM science course, complete the first assignment for Week 11.

Lesson 53

Materials Needed
- *Delightful Reading, Level 3: From Words to Books* Kit (Track A)
- *A Child's Copybook Reader, Volume 1* (Track B)
- *Busy Times*, if needed (Track B)
- Math course of choice

Math: Work on your selected math curriculum for 15–20 minutes.

Track A: Spend 10–15 minutes working on *Delightful Reading, Level 3: From Words to Books*.

Track B: Help your student finish reading aloud *Busy Times*, pages 93–98, "The Golden Rule," if needed.

Have your student carefully copy the phrase of the fable in *A Child's Copybook Reader, Volume 1*, on page 48: "By and by they came to a deep well,". When he has finished the copywork, invite him to spell any word he remembers. Ask him to spell *by*; if he is unsure, allow him to look at the word.

Lesson 54

Materials Needed
- *Delightful Handwriting* teacher book (Track A)
- *Delightful Handwriting* student copybook (Track A)
- *First Steps*, if needed (Track A)
- *A Child's Copybook Reader, Volume 1* (Track B)
- Math course of choice
- SCM science course of choice

Track A: Complete Lesson 27 in *Delightful Handwriting*.

Help your student finish reading aloud *First Steps*, pages 38–46, "I See Something," if needed.

Track B: Have your student carefully copy the next phrase of the fable in *A Child's Copybook Reader, Volume 1*, on page 49: "and one of them looked down into it". When he has finished the copywork, invite him to spell any word he remembers. Ask him to spell *down*; if he is unsure, allow him to look at the word.

Math: Work on your selected math curriculum for 15–20 minutes.

Science: In your SCM science course, complete the second assignment for Week 11.

Lesson 55

Materials Needed
- *Delightful Reading, Level 3: From Words to Books* Kit (Track A)
- *Busy Times* (Track B)
- Math course of choice
- (Optional) *Journaling a Year in Nature* notebooks

Math: Work on your selected math curriculum for 15–20 minutes.

Track A: Spend 10–15 minutes working on *Delightful Reading, Level 3: From Words to Books*.

Track B: Help your student read aloud *Busy Times*, pages 99–105, "Rachel's Candy."

Tip: Don't worry if your student doesn't get through all of pages 99–105. There is a scheduled catch-up time in lesson 57.

Nature Study: Take the whole family outside for nature study.

Lesson 56

Materials Needed
- *Delightful Reading, Level 3: From Words to Books* Kit (Track A)
- *Delightful Handwriting* teacher book (Track A)
- *Delightful Handwriting* student copybook (Track A)
- *A Child's Copybook Reader, Volume 1* (Track B)
- Math course of choice

Track A: Spend 10–15 minutes working on *Delightful Reading, Level 3: From Words to Books*.
Complete Lesson 28 in *Delightful Handwriting*.

Track B: Have your student carefully copy the rest of the sentence in *A Child's Copybook Reader, Volume 1*, beginning on page 50: "and said to the other, 'This looks like a nice cool place." When he has finished the copywork, invite him to spell any word he remembers. Ask him to spell *this*; if he is unsure, allow him to look at the word.

Tip: Point out the beginning quotation marks that signify what the frog said. The student will not put the ending quotation marks in place until he copies the rest of the frog's remark tomorrow.

Math: Work on your selected math curriculum for 15–20 minutes.

Lesson 57

Materials Needed
- *Delightful Handwriting* teacher book (Track A)
- *Delightful Handwriting* student copybook (Track A)
- *First Steps* (Track A)
- *A Child's Copybook Reader, Volume 1* (Track B)
- *Busy Times*, if needed (Track B)
- Math course of choice
- SCM science course of choice

Track A: Complete Lesson 29 in *Delightful Handwriting*.
Help your student read aloud *First Steps*, pages 47–53, "Something for You."

Tip: Don't worry if your student doesn't get all the way through pages 47–53. You will have time to catch up in lesson 59.

Track B: Have your student carefully copy the next sentence of the fable in *A Child's Copybook Reader, Volume 1*, beginning on page 51: "Let us jump in and settle here." When he has finished the copywork, invite him to spell any word he remembers. Ask him to spell *let*; if he is unsure, allow him to look at the word.

Help your student finish reading aloud *Busy Times*, pages 99–105, "Rachel's Candy," if needed.

Math: Work on your selected math curriculum for 15–20 minutes.

Science: In your SCM science course, complete the first assignment for Week 12.

Reminder: Get A Child's Copybook Reader, Volume 2, *for Track B for lesson 67.*

Lesson 58

Materials Needed
- *Delightful Reading, Level 3: From Words to Books* Kit (Track A)
- *A Child's Copybook Reader, Volume 1* (Track B)
- Math course of choice

Math: Work on your selected math curriculum for 15–20 minutes.

Track A: Spend 10–15 minutes working on *Delightful Reading, Level 3: From Words to Books*.

Track B: Use today to catch up on any assigned copywork in *A Child's Copybook Reader, Volume 1*, as needed.

Lesson 59

Materials Needed
- *Delightful Handwriting* teacher book (Track A)
- *Delightful Handwriting* student copybook (Track A)
- *First Steps*, if needed (Track A)
- *A Child's Copybook Reader, Volume 1* (Track B)
- Math course of choice
- SCM science course of choice

Track A: Complete Lesson 30 in *Delightful Handwriting*.
Help your student finish reading aloud *First Steps*, pages 47–53, "Something for You," if needed.

Track B: Help your student read aloud *A Child's Copybook Reader, Volume 1*, page 53.

Math: Work on your selected math curriculum for 15–20 minutes.

Science: In your SCM science course, complete the second assignment for Week 12.

Lesson 60

Materials Needed
- *Delightful Reading, Level 3: From Words to Books* Kit (Track A)
- *Busy Times* (Track B)
- Math course of choice
- (Optional) *Journaling a Year in Nature* notebooks

Math: Work on your selected math curriculum for 15–20 minutes.

Track A: Spend 10–15 minutes working on *Delightful Reading, Level 3: From Words to Books*.

Track B: Help your student read aloud *Busy Times*, pages 106–118, "Andrew and the Cats."

Tip: From this point on, the scheduled catch-up lessons for readings in Busy Times *will be less frequent. If you need more than one lesson time to read through a chapter, simply begin where you left off instead of starting a new chapter at each lesson. The important thing is to go at your student's pace and not frustrate him.*

Nature Study: Take the whole family outside for nature study.

Term 2

(12 weeks; 5 lessons/week)

Term 2 Resources List
- Math course of choice
- Simply Charlotte Mason (SCM) science course of choice
- *Journaling a Year in Nature* notebooks (optional)

Track A
- *Delightful Reading, Level 3: From Words to Books* Kit
- *Delightful Handwriting* teacher book
- *Delightful Handwriting* student copybook
- *First Steps*
- *Days Go By*

Track B
- *A Child's Copybook Reader, Volumes 1 and 2*
- *Busy Times*
- *More Busy Times*

Weekly Schedule *(most weeks)*

	Day One	Day Two	Day Three	Day Four	Day Five
	Math (15–20 min.)	Math (15–20 min.)	Math (15–20 min.)	Math (15–20 min.)	Math (15–20 min.)
	(Nature Study)		Science (15–20 min.)		Science (15–20 min.)
Track A	First Steps (10–15 min.); Delightful Handwriting (5 min.)	Delightful Reading (10–15 min.)	First Steps (10–15 min.); Delightful Handwriting (5 min.)	Delightful Reading (10–15 min.)	Delightful Reading (10–15 min.); Delightful Handwriting (5 min.)
Track B	Copybook Reader (5 min.)	Copybook Reader (5 min.); Busy Times (10–15 min.)	Copybook Reader (5 min.)	Copybook Reader (5 min.)	Busy Times (10–15 min.)

Lesson 61

Materials Needed
- *Delightful Handwriting* teacher book (Track A)
- *Delightful Handwriting* student copybook (Track A)
- *First Steps* (Track A)
- *A Child's Copybook Reader, Volume 1* (Track B)
- Math course of choice
- (Optional) *Journaling a Year in Nature* notebooks

Math: Work on your selected math curriculum for 15–20 minutes.

Track A: Complete Lesson 31 in *Delightful Handwriting*.
Help your student read aloud *First Steps*, pages 54–61, "The Big Wagon."

Tip: From here on, your student will not have a scheduled catch-up day for reading First Steps. *If you need more than one lesson time to read through a chapter, simply begin where you left off instead of starting a new chapter at each lesson. The important thing is to go at your student's pace and not frustrate him.*

Track B: Have your student carefully copy the next phrase of the fable in *A Child's Copybook Reader, Volume 1*, beginning on page 54: "But the other, who had a wiser head on his shoulders,". When he has finished the copywork, invite him to spell any word he remembers. Ask him to spell *other*; if he is unsure, allow him to look at the word.

Nature Study: Take the whole family outside for nature study.

Lesson 62

Materials Needed
- *Delightful Reading, Level 3: From Words to Books* Kit (Track A)
- *A Child's Copybook Reader, Volume 1* (Track B)
- *Busy Times* (Track B)
- Math course of choice

Track A: Spend 10–15 minutes working on *Delightful Reading, Level 3: From Words to Books*.

Track B: Have your student carefully copy the next part of the fable in *A Child's Copybook Reader, Volume 1*, beginning on page 55: "replied, 'Not so fast, my friend. If this well dried up." When he has finished the copywork, invite him to spell any word he remembers. Ask him to spell *my*; if he is unsure, allow him to look at the word.
Help your student read aloud *Busy Times*, pages 119–128, "The Working Bee."

Notes

Math: Work on your selected math curriculum for 15–20 minutes.

Lesson 63

Materials Needed
- *Delightful Handwriting* teacher book (Track A)
- *Delightful Handwriting* student copybook (Track A)
- *First Steps* (Track A)
- *A Child's Copybook Reader, Volume 1* (Track B)
- Math course of choice
- SCM science course of choice

Track A: Complete Lesson 32 in *Delightful Handwriting*.
    Help your student read aloud *First Steps*, pages 62–70, "The Little Table."

Track B: Have your student carefully copy the rest of the sentence in *A Child's Copybook Reader, Volume 1*, beginning on page 57: "like the marsh, how should we get out again?" When he has finished the copywork, invite him to spell any word he remembers. Ask him to spell *out*; if he is unsure, allow him to look at the word.

Math: Work on your selected math curriculum for 15–20 minutes.

Science: In your SCM science course, complete the first assignment for Week 13.

Lesson 64

Materials Needed
- *Delightful Reading, Level 3: From Words to Books* Kit (Track A)
- *A Child's Copybook Reader, Volume 1* (Track B)
- Math course of choice

Math: Work on your selected math curriculum for 15–20 minutes.

Track A: Spend 10–15 minutes working on *Delightful Reading, Level 3: From Words to Books*.

Track B: Have your student carefully copy the moral of the fable in *A Child's Copybook Reader, Volume 1*, beginning on page 58: "Moral: Think twice before you act." When he has finished the copywork, invite him to spell any word he remembers. Ask him to spell *think*; if he is unsure, allow him to look at the word.

Lesson 65

Materials Needed
- *Delightful Handwriting* teacher book (Track A)

- *Delightful Handwriting* student copybook (Track A)
- *Delightful Reading, Level 3: From Words to Books* Kit (Track A)
- *Busy Times* (Track B)
- Math course of choice
- SCM science course of choice

Track A: Spend 10–15 minutes working on *Delightful Reading, Level 3: From Words to Books.*
    Complete Lesson 33 in *Delightful Handwriting.*

Track B: Help your student read aloud *Busy Times,* pages 130–137, "The Only Girl."

Math: Work on your selected math curriculum for 15–20 minutes.

Science: In your SCM science course, complete the second assignment for Week 13.

Lesson 66

Materials Needed
- *Delightful Handwriting* teacher book (Track A)
- *Delightful Handwriting* student copybook (Track A)
- *First Steps* (Track A)
- *A Child's Copybook Reader, Volume 1* (Track B)
- Math course of choice
- (Optional) *Journaling a Year in Nature* notebooks

Math: Work on your selected math curriculum for 15–20 minutes.

Track A: Complete Lesson 34 in *Delightful Handwriting.*
    Help your student read aloud *First Steps,* pages 71–78, "The Colt."

Track B: Help your student read the fable in *A Child's Copybook Reader, Volume 1,* page 60. If desired, review 6–10 of these words and his selected words from previous copywork lessons: *two, but, look, get, by, down, this, let, other, my, out, think.* If your student is unsure about a particular word's spelling, allow him to look at the word.

Nature Study: Take the whole family outside for nature study.

Lesson 67

Materials Needed
- *Delightful Reading, Level 3: From Words to Books* Kit (Track A)
- *A Child's Copybook Reader, Volume 2* (Track B)
- *Busy Times,* as needed (Track B)
- Math course of choice

Track A: Spend 10–15 minutes working on *Delightful Reading, Level 3: From Words to Books.*

Track B: Have your student read aloud the stanza in *A Child's Copybook Reader, Volume 2*, on page 4, then carefully copy page 5. When he has finished the copywork, invite him to spell any word he remembers. Ask him to spell *its*; if he is unsure, allow him to look at the word.

Use today to catch up on any assigned reading from *Busy Times*, as needed.

Math: Work on your selected math curriculum for 15–20 minutes.

Lesson 68

Materials Needed
- *Delightful Handwriting* teacher book (Track A)
- *Delightful Handwriting* student copybook (Track A)
- *First Steps* (Track A)
- *A Child's Copybook Reader, Volume 2* (Track B)
- Math course of choice
- SCM science course of choice

Track A: Complete Lesson 35 in *Delightful Handwriting*.
Help your student read aloud *First Steps*, pages 79–88, "What Can I Do?"

Track B: Have your student carefully copy *A Child's Copybook Reader, Volume 2*, page 6. When he has finished the copywork, invite him to spell any word he remembers. Ask him to spell *go*; if he is unsure, allow him to look at the word.

Math: Work on your selected math curriculum for 15–20 minutes.

Science: In your SCM science course, complete the first assignment for Week 14.

Lesson 69

Materials Needed
- *Delightful Reading, Level 3: From Words to Books* Kit (Track A)
- *A Child's Copybook Reader, Volume 2* (Track B)
- Math course of choice

Math: Work on your selected math curriculum for 15–20 minutes.

Track A: Spend 10–15 minutes working on *Delightful Reading, Level 3: From Words to Books*.

Track B: Have your student read aloud the stanza in *A Child's Copybook Reader, Volume 2*, on page 7, then carefully copy page 8. When he has finished the copywork, invite him to spell any word he remembers. Ask him to spell *was*; if he is unsure, allow him to look at the word.

Lesson 70

Materials Needed
- *Delightful Handwriting* teacher book (Track A)
- *Delightful Handwriting* student copybook (Track A)
- *Delightful Reading, Level 3: From Words to Books* Kit (Track A)
- *Busy Times* (Track B)
- Math course of choice
- SCM science course of choice

Track A: Spend 10–15 minutes working on *Delightful Reading, Level 3: From Words to Books.*
   Complete Lesson 36 in *Delightful Handwriting.*

Track B: Help your student read aloud *Busy Times*, pages 138–143, "Getting Ready to Move."

Math: Work on your selected math curriculum for 15–20 minutes.

Science: In your SCM science course, complete the second assignment for Week 14.

Lesson 71

Materials Needed
- *Delightful Handwriting* teacher book (Track A)
- *Delightful Handwriting* student copybook (Track A)
- *First Steps* (Track A)
- *A Child's Copybook Reader, Volume 2* (Track B)
- Math course of choice
- (Optional) *Journaling a Year in Nature* notebooks

Math: Work on your selected math curriculum for 15–20 minutes.

Track A: Complete Lesson 37 in *Delightful Handwriting.*
   Help your student read aloud *First Steps*, pages 89–94, "To the Store."

Track B: Have your student carefully copy *A Child's Copybook Reader, Volume 2*, page 9. When he has finished the copywork, invite him to spell any word he remembers. Ask him to spell *play*; if he is unsure, allow him to look at the word.

Nature Study: Take the whole family outside for nature study.

Lesson 72

Materials Needed
- *Delightful Reading, Level 3: From Words to Books* Kit (Track A)
- *A Child's Copybook Reader, Volume 2* (Track B)

- *Busy Times* (Track B)
- Math course of choice

Track A: Spend 10–15 minutes working on *Delightful Reading, Level 3: From Words to Books*.

Track B: Have your student read aloud the stanza in *A Child's Copybook Reader, Volume 2*, on page 10, then carefully copy page 11. When he has finished the copywork, invite him to spell any word he remembers. Ask him to spell *so*; if he is unsure, allow him to look at the word.
    Help your student read aloud *Busy Times*, pages 144–154, "A Busy Day."

Math: Work on your selected math curriculum for 15–20 minutes.

Lesson 73

Materials Needed
- *Delightful Handwriting* teacher book (Track A)
- *Delightful Handwriting* student copybook (Track A)
- *First Steps* (Track A)
- *A Child's Copybook Reader, Volume 2* (Track B)
- Math course of choice
- SCM science course of choice

Track A: Complete Lesson 38 in *Delightful Handwriting*.
    Help your student read aloud *First Steps*, pages 95–102, "Something Good."

Track B: Have your student carefully copy *A Child's Copybook Reader, Volume 2*, page 12. When he has finished the copywork, invite him to spell any word he remembers. Ask him to spell *about*; if he is unsure, allow him to look at the word.

Math: Work on your selected math curriculum for 15–20 minutes.

Science: In your SCM science course, complete the first assignment for Week 15.

Lesson 74

Materials Needed
- *Delightful Reading, Level 3: From Words to Books* Kit (Track A)
- *A Child's Copybook Reader, Volume 2* (Track B)
- Math course of choice

Math: Work on your selected math curriculum for 15–20 minutes.

Track A: Spend 10–15 minutes working on *Delightful Reading, Level 3: From Words to Books*.

Track B: Have your student read aloud the stanza in *A Child's Copybook Reader, Volume 2*, on page 13, then carefully copy page 14. When he has finished the copywork, invite him to spell any word he remembers. Ask him to spell *her*; if he is unsure, allow him to look at the word.

Lesson 75

Materials Needed
- *Delightful Handwriting* teacher book (Track A)
- *Delightful Handwriting* student copybook (Track A)
- *Delightful Reading, Level 3: From Words to Books* Kit (Track A)
- *Busy Times* (Track B)
- Math course of choice
- SCM science course of choice

Track A: Spend 10–15 minutes working on *Delightful Reading, Level 3: From Words to Books*.
   Complete Lesson 39 in *Delightful Handwriting*.

Track B: Help your student read aloud *Busy Times*, pages 155–166, "The Long Ride."

Math: Work on your selected math curriculum for 15–20 minutes.

Science: In your SCM science course, complete the second assignment for Week 15.

Lesson 76

Materials Needed
- *Delightful Handwriting* teacher book (Track A)
- *Delightful Handwriting* student copybook (Track A)
- *First Steps* (Track A)
- *A Child's Copybook Reader, Volume 2* (Track B)
- Math course of choice
- (Optional) *Journaling a Year in Nature* notebooks

Math: Work on your selected math curriculum for 15–20 minutes.

Track A: Complete Lesson 40 in *Delightful Handwriting*.
   Help your student read aloud *First Steps*, pages 103–108, "One, Two, Three."

Track B: Have your student carefully copy *A Child's Copybook Reader, Volume 2*, page 15. When he has finished the copywork, invite him to spell any word he remembers. Ask him to spell *said*; if he is unsure, allow him to look at the word.

Nature Study: Take the whole family outside for nature study.

Notes

Lesson 77

Materials Needed
- *Delightful Reading, Level 3: From Words to Books* Kit (Track A)
- *A Child's Copybook Reader, Volume 2* (Track B)
- *Busy Times*, as needed (Track B)
- Math course of choice

Track A: Spend 10–15 minutes working on *Delightful Reading, Level 3: From Words to Books.*

Track B: Have your student read aloud the stanza in *A Child's Copybook Reader, Volume 2*, on page 16, then carefully copy page 17. When he has finished the copywork, invite him to spell any word he remembers. Ask him to spell *love*; if he is unsure, allow him to look at the word.

Use today to catch up on any assigned reading from *Busy Times*, as needed.

Math: Work on your selected math curriculum for 15–20 minutes.

Lesson 78

Materials Needed
- *Delightful Handwriting* teacher book (Track A)
- *Delightful Handwriting* student copybook (Track A)
- *First Steps* (Track A)
- *A Child's Copybook Reader, Volume 2* (Track B)
- Math course of choice
- SCM science course of choice

Track A: Complete Lesson 41 in *Delightful Handwriting*.
Help your student read aloud *First Steps*, pages 109–117, "Rain, Rain, Rain."

Track B: Have your student carefully copy *A Child's Copybook Reader, Volume 2*, page 18. When he has finished the copywork, invite him to spell any word he remembers. Ask him to spell *did*; if he is unsure, allow him to look at the word.

Math: Work on your selected math curriculum for 15–20 minutes.

Science: In your SCM science course, complete the first assignment for Week 16.

Reminder: Get Days Go By *for Track A for lesson 88.*

Lesson 79

Materials Needed
- *Delightful Reading, Level 3: From Words to Books* Kit (Track A)
- *A Child's Copybook Reader, Volume 2* (Track B)

- Math course of choice

Math: Work on your selected math curriculum for 15–20 minutes.

Track A: Spend 10–15 minutes working on *Delightful Reading, Level 3: From Words to Books*.

Track B: Have your student read aloud the stanza in *A Child's Copybook Reader, Volume 2*, on page 19, then carefully copy page 20. When he has finished the copywork, invite him to spell any word he remembers. Ask him to spell *you*; if he is unsure, allow him to look at the word.

Lesson 80

Materials Needed
- *Delightful Handwriting* teacher book (Track A)
- *Delightful Handwriting* student copybook (Track A)
- *Delightful Reading, Level 3: From Words to Books* Kit (Track A)
- *Busy Times* (Track B)
- Math course of choice
- SCM science course of choice

Track A: Spend 10–15 minutes working on *Delightful Reading, Level 3: From Words to Books*.
    Complete Lesson 42 in *Delightful Handwriting*.

Track B: Help your student read aloud *Busy Times*, pages 167–179, "The New Farm."

Math: Work on your selected math curriculum for 15–20 minutes.

Science: In your SCM science course, complete the second assignment for Week 16.

Lesson 81

Materials Needed
- *Delightful Handwriting* teacher book (Track A)
- *Delightful Handwriting* student copybook (Track A)
- *First Steps* (Track A)
- *A Child's Copybook Reader, Volume 2* (Track B)
- Math course of choice
- (Optional) *Journaling a Year in Nature* notebooks

Math: Work on your selected math curriculum for 15–20 minutes.

Track A: Complete Lesson 43 in *Delightful Handwriting*.
    Help your student read aloud *First Steps*, pages 118–123, "A Name for the Colt."

Track B: Have your student carefully copy *A Child's Copybook Reader, Volume 2*, page 21. When he has finished the copywork, invite him to spell any word he remembers. Ask him to spell *make*; if he is unsure, allow him to look at the word. See if he can also spell *call*.

Nature Study: Take the whole family outside for nature study.

Lesson 82

Materials Needed
- *Delightful Reading, Level 3: From Words to Books* Kit (Track A)
- *Delightful Handwriting* teacher book (Track A)
- *Delightful Handwriting* student copybook (Track A)
- *A Child's Copybook Reader, Volume 2* (Track B)
- Math course of choice

Track A: Spend 10–15 minutes working on *Delightful Reading, Level 3: From Words to Books*.
  Complete Lesson 44 in *Delightful Handwriting*.

Track B: Have your student read aloud "Mary's Lamb" from *A Child's Copybook Reader, Volume 2*, page 22. If desired, review 6–10 of these words and his selected words from previous copywork lessons: *its, go, was, play, so, about, her, said, did, you, make, call*. If your student is unsure about a particular word's spelling, allow him to look at the word.

Math: Work on your selected math curriculum for 15–20 minutes.

Lesson 83

Materials Needed
- *First Steps* (Track A)
- *Busy Times* (Track B)
- Math course of choice
- SCM science course of choice

Track A: Help your student read aloud *First Steps*, pages 124–131, "Peter Finds a Name."

Track B: Help your student read aloud *Busy Times*, pages 180–189, "An Evening with Peter and Rachel."

Math: Work on your selected math curriculum for 15–20 minutes.

Science: In your SCM science course, complete the first assignment for Week 17.

Lesson 84

Materials Needed
- *Delightful Reading, Level 3: From Words to Books* Kit (Track A)
- *Delightful Handwriting* teacher book (Track A)
- *Delightful Handwriting* student copybook (Track A)
- *A Child's Copybook Reader, Volume 2* (Track B)
- Math course of choice

Math: Work on your selected math curriculum for 15–20 minutes.

Track A: Spend 10–15 minutes working on *Delightful Reading, Level 3: From Words to Books*.
Complete Lesson 45 in *Delightful Handwriting*.

Track B: Have your student read aloud the paragraph in *A Child's Copybook Reader, Volume 2*, on page 24, then carefully copy the first two sentences of the story, beginning on page 25: "Hal Smith has a big farm. He has lofts filled with apples and barns filled with barley." When he has finished the copywork, invite him to spell any word he remembers. Ask him to spell *with*; if he is unsure, allow him to look at the word.

Lesson 85

Materials Needed
- *Delightful Reading, Level 3: From Words to Books* Kit (Track A)
- *Delightful Handwriting* teacher book (Track A)
- *Delightful Handwriting* student copybook (Track A)
- *Busy Times* (Track B)
- Math course of choice
- SCM science course of choice

Track A: Spend 10–15 minutes working on *Delightful Reading, Level 3: From Words to Books*.
Complete Lesson 46 in *Delightful Handwriting*.

Track B: Help your student read aloud *Busy Times*, pages 190–198, "Home at Last."

Math: Work on your selected math curriculum for 15–20 minutes.

Science: In your SCM science course, complete the second assignment for Week 17.

Lesson 86

Materials Needed
- *Delightful Handwriting* teacher book (Track A)
- *Delightful Handwriting* student copybook (Track A)
- *First Steps* (Track A)

Notes

- *A Child's Copybook Reader, Volume 2* (Track B)
- Math course of choice
- (Optional) *Journaling a Year in Nature* notebooks

Math: Work on your selected math curriculum for 15–20 minutes.

Track A: Complete Lesson 47 in *Delightful Handwriting*.
　　Help your student read aloud *First Steps*, pages 132–140, "Come and Play Store."

Track B: Have your student carefully copy the next sentence of the story in *A Child's Copybook Reader, Volume 2*, beginning on page 26: "He has a windmill on the top of the hill and a garden at the bottom of it." When he has finished the copywork, invite him to spell any word he remembers. Ask him to spell *on*; if he is unsure, allow him to look at the word.

Nature Study: Take the whole family outside for nature study.

Lesson 87

Materials Needed
- *Delightful Reading, Level 3: From Words to Books* Kit (Track A)
- *Delightful Handwriting* teacher book (Track A)
- *Delightful Handwriting* student copybook (Track A)
- *A Child's Copybook Reader, Volume 2* (Track B)
- *Busy Times*, if needed (Track B)
- Math course of choice

Track A: Spend 10–15 minutes working on *Delightful Reading, Level 3: From Words to Books*.
　　Complete Lesson 48 in *Delightful Handwriting*.

Track B: Have your student carefully copy the next sentence of the story in *A Child's Copybook Reader, Volume 2*, beginning on page 27: "In his farmyard he has hens and chickens, cocks and ducks, pigs and dogs." When he has finished the copywork, invite him to spell any word he remembers. Ask him to spell *his*; if he is unsure, allow him to look at the word.
　　Use today to catch up on any assigned reading in *Busy Times*, as needed.

Math: Work on your selected math curriculum for 15–20 minutes.

Lesson 88

Materials Needed
- *Days Go By* (Track A)
- *A Child's Copybook Reader, Volume 2* (Track B)
- Math course of choice
- SCM science course of choice

Track A: Help your student read aloud *Days Go By*, pages 6–14, "Levi and Susan."

Tip: If the story is too long for your beginning reader, you might take turns reading a page each.

Track B: Have your student read aloud the paragraph in *A Child's Copybook Reader, Volume 2*, on page 29, then carefully copy the first sentence on page 30: "Hal has six boys." When he has finished the copywork, invite him to spell any word he remembers. Ask him to spell *boys*; if he is unsure, allow him to look at the word.

Math: Work on your selected math curriculum for 15–20 minutes.

Science: In your SCM science course, complete the first assignment for Week 18.

Lesson 89

Materials Needed
- *Delightful Reading, Level 3: From Words to Books* Kit (Track A)
- *Delightful Handwriting* teacher book (Track A)
- *Delightful Handwriting* student copybook (Track A)
- *A Child's Copybook Reader, Volume 2* (Track B)
- Math course of choice

Math: Work on your selected math curriculum for 15–20 minutes.

Track A: Spend 10–15 minutes working on *Delightful Reading, Level 3: From Words to Books*.
   Complete Lesson 49 in *Delightful Handwriting*.

Track B: Have your student carefully copy the next sentence of the story in *A Child's Copybook Reader, Volume 2*, beginning on page 30: "They are strong and willing, and help their Daddy as much as they can." When he has finished the copywork, invite him to spell any word he remembers. Ask him to spell *are*; if he is unsure, allow him to look at the word. See if he can also spell *they*.

Lesson 90

Materials Needed
- *Delightful Reading, Level 3: From Words to Books* Kit (Track A)
- *Delightful Handwriting* teacher book (Track A)
- *Delightful Handwriting* student copybook (Track A)
- *Busy Times* (Track B)
- Math course of choice
- SCM science course of choice

Notes

Track A: Spend 10–15 minutes working on *Delightful Reading, Level 3: From Words to Books*.

Complete Lesson 50 in *Delightful Handwriting*.

Track B: Help your student read aloud *Busy Times*, pages 200–209, "We Want a Pony."

Math: Work on your selected math curriculum for 15–20 minutes.

Science: In your SCM science course, complete the second assignment for Week 18.

Lesson 91

Materials Needed
- *Delightful Handwriting* teacher book (Track A)
- *Delightful Handwriting* student copybook (Track A)
- *Days Go By* (Track A)
- *A Child's Copybook Reader, Volume 2* (Track B)
- Math course of choice
- (Optional) *Journaling a Year in Nature* notebooks

Math: Work on your selected math curriculum for 15–20 minutes.

Track A: Complete Lesson 51 in *Delightful Handwriting*.

Help your student read aloud *Days Go By*, pages 15–22, "A Doll for Susan."

Track B: Have your student carefully copy the next sentence of the story in *A Child's Copybook Reader, Volume 2*, beginning on page 31: "Mark is the eldest; he goes with the cart to the mill." When he has finished the copywork, invite him to spell any word he remembers. Ask him to spell *cart*; if he is unsure, allow him to look at the word.

Tip: If desired, point out the semicolon and how it connects two complete sentences.

Nature Study: Take the whole family outside for nature study.

Lesson 92

Materials Needed
- *Delightful Reading, Level 3: From Words to Books* Kit (Track A)
- *Delightful Handwriting* teacher book (Track A)
- *Delightful Handwriting* student copybook (Track A)
- *A Child's Copybook Reader, Volume 2* (Track B)
- *Busy Times* (Track B)
- Math course of choice

Track A: Spend 10–15 minutes working on *Delightful Reading, Level 3: From Words to Books*.

Complete Lesson 52 in *Delightful Handwriting*.

Track B: Have your student carefully copy the next sentence of the story in *A Child's Copybook Reader, Volume 2*, beginning on page 32: "Timothy is the next; he thrashes the barley in the barn." When he has finished the copywork, invite him to spell any word he remembers. Ask him to spell *he*; if he is unsure, allow him to look at the word.

Help your student read aloud *Busy Times*, pages 210–222, "The New Bat."

Math: Work on your selected math curriculum for 15–20 minutes.

Reminder: Get More Busy Times *for Track B for lesson 102.*

Lesson 93

Materials Needed
- *Days Go By* (Track A)
- *A Child's Copybook Reader, Volume 2* (Track B)
- Math course of choice
- SCM science course of choice

Track A: Help your student read aloud *Days Go By*, pages 23–27, "A Doll in the Tree."

Track B: Have your student read aloud the paragraph in *A Child's Copybook Reader, Volume 2*, on page 34, then carefully copy the first sentence, beginning on page 35: "Martin is the next; he goes to market to sell the eggs and milk." When he has finished the copywork, invite him to spell any word he remembers. Ask him to spell *to*; if he is unsure, allow him to look at the word.

Math: Work on your selected math curriculum for 15–20 minutes.

Science: In your SCM science course, complete the first assignment for Week 19.

Lesson 94

Materials Needed
- *Delightful Reading, Level 3: From Words to Books* Kit (Track A)
- *Delightful Handwriting* teacher book (Track A)
- *Delightful Handwriting* student copybook (Track A)
- *A Child's Copybook Reader, Volume 2* (Track B)
- Math course of choice

Math: Work on your selected math curriculum for 15–20 minutes.

Track A: Spend 10–15 minutes working on *Delightful Reading, Level 3: From Words to Books*.

Complete Lesson 53 in *Delightful Handwriting*.

Track B: Have your student carefully copy the next sentence of the story in *A Child's Copybook Reader, Volume 2*, on page 36: "Bill is the next; he digs in the garden." When he has finished the copywork, invite him to spell any word he remembers. Ask him to spell *digs*; if he is unsure, allow him to look at the word.

Lesson 95

Materials Needed
- *Delightful Reading, Level 3: From Words to Books* Kit (Track A)
- *Delightful Handwriting* teacher book (Track A)
- *Delightful Handwriting* student copybook (Track A)
- *Busy Times* (Track B)
- Math course of choice
- SCM science course of choice

Track A: Spend 10–15 minutes working on *Delightful Reading, Level 3: From Words to Books*.

Complete Lesson 54 in *Delightful Handwriting*.

Track B: Help your student read aloud *Busy Times*, pages 223–232, "Who Broke the Bat?"

Math: Work on your selected math curriculum for 15–20 minutes.

Science: In your SCM science course, complete the second assignment for Week 19.

Lesson 96

Materials Needed
- *Delightful Handwriting* teacher book (Track A)
- *Delightful Handwriting* student copybook (Track A)
- *Days Go By* (Track A)
- *A Child's Copybook Reader, Volume 2* (Track B)
- Math course of choice
- (Optional) *Journaling a Year in Nature* notebooks

Math: Work on your selected math curriculum for 15–20 minutes.

Track A: Complete Lesson 55 in *Delightful Handwriting*.

Help your student read aloud *Days Go By*, pages 28–36, "Blackie Comes Down."

Track B: Have your student carefully copy the next sentence of the story in *A Child's Copybook Reader, Volume 2*, beginning on page 36: "Charley is the next; he gives the pigs their slop, and the chickens their crumbs." When he has finished the copywork, invite him to spell any word he remembers. Ask him to spell *pigs*; if he is unsure, allow him to look at the word.

Nature Study: Take the whole family outside for nature study.

Lesson 97

Materials Needed
- *Delightful Reading, Level 3: From Words to Books* Kit (Track A)
- *Delightful Handwriting* teacher book (Track A)
- *Delightful Handwriting* student copybook (Track A)
- *A Child's Copybook Reader, Volume 2* (Track B)
- *Busy Times* (Track B)
- Math course of choice

Track A: Spend 10–15 minutes working on *Delightful Reading, Level 3: From Words to Books*.
　　Complete Lesson 56 in *Delightful Handwriting*.

Track B: Have your student carefully copy the next sentence of the story in *A Child's Copybook Reader, Volume 2*, on page 38: "Josh is the last." When he has finished the copywork, invite him to spell any word he remembers. Ask him to spell *last*; if he is unsure, allow him to look at the word.
　　Help your student read aloud *Busy Times*, pages 233–245, "Nancy Makes Things Right."

Math: Work on your selected math curriculum for 15–20 minutes.

Lesson 98

Materials Needed
- *Days Go By* (Track A)
- *A Child's Copybook Reader, Volume 2* (Track B)
- Math course of choice
- SCM science course of choice

Track A: Help your student read aloud *Days Go By*, pages 37–42, "A Happy Time."

Track B: Have your student carefully copy the last sentence of the story in *A Child's Copybook Reader, Volume 2*, beginning on page 38: "He is so little that he cannot do much yet, but he runs on errands very willingly." When he has finished the copywork, invite him to spell any word he remembers. Ask him to spell *do*; if he is unsure, allow him to look at the word. See if he can also spell *much*.

Math: Work on your selected math curriculum for 15–20 minutes.

Notes

Science: In your SCM science course, complete the first assignment for Week 20.

Lesson 99

Materials Needed
- *Delightful Reading, Level 3: From Words to Books* Kit (Track A)
- *Delightful Handwriting* teacher book (Track A)
- *Delightful Handwriting* student copybook (Track A)
- *A Child's Copybook Reader, Volume 2* (Track B)
- Math course of choice

Math: Work on your selected math curriculum for 15–20 minutes.

Track A: Spend 10–15 minutes working on *Delightful Reading, Level 3: From Words to Books*.
     Complete Lesson 57 in *Delightful Handwriting*.

Track B: Have your student read aloud the story in *A Child's Copybook Reader, Volume 2*, on page 40. If desired, review 6–10 of these words and his selected words from previous copywork lessons: *with, on, his, boys, they, are, cart, he, to, digs, pigs, last, do, much*. If your student is unsure about a particular word's spelling, allow him to look at the word.

Lesson 100

Materials Needed
- *Delightful Reading, Level 3: From Words to Books* Kit (Track A)
- *Delightful Handwriting* teacher book (Track A)
- *Delightful Handwriting* student copybook (Track A)
- *Busy Times*, if needed (Track B)
- Math course of choice
- SCM science course of choice

Track A: Spend 10–15 minutes working on *Delightful Reading, Level 3: From Words to Books*.
     Complete Lesson 58 in *Delightful Handwriting*.

Track B: Use today to catch up on any assigned reading in *Busy Times*, as needed.

Math: Work on your selected math curriculum for 15–20 minutes.

Science: In your SCM science course, complete the second assignment for Week 20.

Lesson 101

Materials Needed
- *Delightful Handwriting* teacher book (Track A)
- *Delightful Handwriting* student copybook (Track A)
- *Days Go By* (Track A)
- *A Child's Copybook Reader, Volume 2* (Track B)
- Math course of choice
- (Optional) *Journaling a Year in Nature* notebooks

Math: Work on your selected math curriculum for 15–20 minutes.

Track A: Complete Lesson 59 in *Delightful Handwriting*.
  Help your student read aloud *Days Go By*, pages 44–50, "Prince."

Track B: Have your student read aloud *A Child's Copybook Reader, Volume 2*, page 42.

Nature Study: Take the whole family outside for nature study.

Lesson 102

Materials Needed
- *Delightful Reading, Level 3: From Words to Books* Kit (Track A)
- *Delightful Handwriting* teacher book (Track A)
- *Delightful Handwriting* student copybook (Track A)
- *A Child's Copybook Reader, Volume 2* (Track B)
- *More Busy Times* (Track B)
- Math course of choice

Track A: Spend 10–15 minutes working on *Delightful Reading, Level 3: From Words to Books*.
  Complete Lesson 60 in *Delightful Handwriting*.

Track B: Have your student carefully copy the first part of the Scripture passage in *A Child's Copybook Reader, Volume 2*, page 43: "Everyone then who hears these words of mine and does them." When he has finished the copywork, invite him to spell any word he remembers. Ask him to spell *then*; if he is unsure, allow him to look at the word.
  Help your student read aloud *More Busy Times*, pages 6–15, "What's Wrong with Rachel?"

Math: Work on your selected math curriculum for 15–20 minutes.

Lesson 103

Materials Needed
- *Days Go By* (Track A)
- *A Child's Copybook Reader, Volume 2* (Track B)

Notes

- Math course of choice
- SCM science course of choice

Track A: Help your student read aloud *Days Go By*, pages 51–58, "No Ride for Peter."

Track B: Have your student carefully copy the rest of the sentence in *A Child's Copybook Reader, Volume 2*, on page 44: "will be like a wise man who built his house on the rock." When he has finished the copywork, invite him to spell any word he remembers. Ask him to spell *who*; if he is unsure, allow him to look at the word.

Math: Work on your selected math curriculum for 15–20 minutes.

Science: In your SCM science course, complete the first assignment for Week 21.

Lesson 104

Materials Needed
- *Delightful Reading, Level 3: From Words to Books* Kit (Track A)
- *Delightful Handwriting* teacher book (Track A)
- *Delightful Handwriting* student copybook (Track A)
- *A Child's Copybook Reader, Volume 2* (Track B)
- Math course of choice

Math: Work on your selected math curriculum for 15–20 minutes.

Track A: Spend 10–15 minutes working on *Delightful Reading, Level 3: From Words to Books*.
Complete Lesson 61 in *Delightful Handwriting*.

Track B: Have your student carefully copy the first part of the next sentence of the Scripture passage in *A Child's Copybook Reader, Volume 2*, beginning on page 45: "And the rain fell, and the floods came, and the winds blew and beat on that house,". When he has finished the copywork, invite him to spell any word he remembers. Ask him to spell *rain*; if he is unsure, allow him to look at the word.

Lesson 105

Materials Needed
- *Delightful Reading, Level 3: From Words to Books* Kit (Track A)
- *Delightful Handwriting* teacher book (Track A)
- *Delightful Handwriting* student copybook (Track A)
- *More Busy Times* (Track B)
- Math course of choice
- SCM science course of choice

Track A: Spend 10–15 minutes working on *Delightful Reading, Level 3: From Words to Books.*

Complete Lesson 62 in *Delightful Handwriting.*

Track B: Help your student read aloud *More Busy Times*, pages 16–26, "Peter's Plan."

Math: Work on your selected math curriculum for 15–20 minutes.

Science: In your SCM science course, complete the second assignment for Week 21.

Lesson 106

Materials Needed
- *Delightful Handwriting* teacher book (Track A)
- *Delightful Handwriting* student copybook (Track A)
- *Days Go By* (Track A)
- *A Child's Copybook Reader, Volume 2* (Track B)
- Math course of choice
- (Optional) *Journaling a Year in Nature* notebooks

Math: Work on your selected math curriculum for 15–20 minutes.

Track A: Complete Lesson 63 in *Delightful Handwriting.*

Help your student read aloud *Days Go By*, pages 59–64, "We Want a Dog."

Track B: Have your student carefully copy the rest of the sentence in *A Child's Copybook Reader, Volume 2*, beginning on page 46: "but it did not fall, because it had been founded on the rock." When he has finished the copywork, invite him to spell any word he remembers. Ask him to spell *been*; if he is unsure, allow him to look at the word. See if he can also spell *rock*.

Nature Study: Take the whole family outside for nature study.

Lesson 107

Materials Needed
- *Delightful Reading, Level 3: From Words to Books* Kit (Track A)
- *Delightful Handwriting* teacher book (Track A)
- *Delightful Handwriting* student copybook (Track A)
- *More Busy Times* (Track B)
- Math course of choice

Track A: Spend 10–15 minutes working on *Delightful Reading, Level 3: From Words to Books.*

Complete Lesson 64 in *Delightful Handwriting.*

Track B: Help your student read aloud *More Busy Times*, pages 27–38, "A Special Day."

Math: Work on your selected math curriculum for 15–20 minutes.

Lesson 108

Materials Needed
- *Days Go By* (Track A)
- *A Child's Copybook Reader, Volume 2* (Track B)
- Math course of choice
- SCM science course of choice

Track A: Help your student read aloud *Days Go By*, pages 65–70, "Just One Dog."

Track B: Have your student read aloud *A Child's Copybook Reader, Volume 2*, page 48, then carefully copy the first part of the next sentence in the Scripture passage, beginning on page 49: "And everyone who hears these words of mind and does not do them." When he has finished the copywork, invite him to spell any word he remembers. Ask him to spell *words*; if he is unsure, allow him to look at the word.

Math: Work on your selected math curriculum for 15–20 minutes.

Science: In your SCM science course, complete the first assignment for Week 22.

Lesson 109

Materials Needed
- *Delightful Reading, Level 3: From Words to Books* Kit (Track A)
- *Delightful Handwriting* teacher book (Track A)
- *Delightful Handwriting* student copybook (Track A)
- *A Child's Copybook Reader, Volume 2* (Track B)
- Math course of choice

Math: Work on your selected math curriculum for 15–20 minutes.

Track A: Spend 10–15 minutes working on *Delightful Reading, Level 3: From Words to Books*.
   Complete Lesson 65 in *Delightful Handwriting*.

Track B: Have your student carefully copy the rest of the sentence in *A Child's Copybook Reader, Volume 2*, beginning on page 50: "will be like a foolish man who built his house on the sand." When he has finished the copywork, invite him to spell any word he remembers. Ask him to spell *will*; if he is unsure, allow him to look at the word.

Lesson 110

Materials Needed
- *Delightful Reading, Level 3: From Words to Books* Kit (Track A)
- *Delightful Handwriting* teacher book (Track A)
- *Delightful Handwriting* student copybook (Track A)
- *More Busy Times* (Track B)
- Math course of choice
- SCM science course of choice

Track A: Spend 10–15 minutes working on *Delightful Reading, Level 3: From Words to Books*.
Complete Lesson 66 in *Delightful Handwriting*.

Track B: Help your student read aloud *More Busy Times*, pages 39–50, "Grandfather Plays Doctor."

Math: Work on your selected math curriculum for 15–20 minutes.

Science: In your SCM science course, complete the second assignment for Week 22.

Lesson 111

Materials Needed
- *Delightful Handwriting* teacher book (Track A)
- *Delightful Handwriting* student copybook (Track A)
- *Days Go By* (Track A)
- *A Child's Copybook Reader, Volume 2* (Track B)
- Math course of choice
- (Optional) *Journaling a Year in Nature* notebooks

Math: Work on your selected math curriculum for 15–20 minutes.

Track A: Complete Lesson 67 in *Delightful Handwriting*.
Help your student read aloud *Days Go By*, pages 71–76, "The Lost Puppy."

Track B: Have your student carefully copy the first part of the next sentence of the Scripture passage in *A Child's Copybook Reader, Volume 2*, beginning on page 51: "And the rain fell, an the floods came, and the winds blew and beat against that house." When he has finished the copywork, invite him to spell any word he remembers. Ask him to spell *came*; if he is unsure, allow him to look at the word.

Nature Study: Take the whole family outside for nature study.

Reminder: Get A Child's Copybook Reader, Volume 3, *for Track B for lesson 121.*

Lesson 112

Materials Needed
- *Delightful Reading, Level 3: From Words to Books* Kit (Track A)
- *Delightful Handwriting* teacher book (Track A)
- *Delightful Handwriting* student copybook (Track A)
- *A Child's Copybook Reader, Volume 2* (Track B)
- *More Busy Times*, if needed (Track B)
- Math course of choice

Track A: Spend 10–15 minutes working on *Delightful Reading, Level 3: From Words to Books*.
Complete Lesson 68 in *Delightful Handwriting*.

Track B: Have your student carefully copy the rest of the sentence in *A Child's Copybook Reader, Volume 2*, beginning on page 52: "and it fell, and great was the fall of it." When he has finished the copywork, invite him to spell any word he remembers. Ask him to spell *fall*; if he is unsure, allow him to look at the word. See if he can also spell *fell*.
Use today to catch up on any assigned reading in *More Busy Times*, as needed.

Math: Work on your selected math curriculum for 15–20 minutes.

Lesson 113

Materials Needed
- *Days Go By* (Track A)
- *A Child's Copybook Reader, Volume 2* (Track B)
- Math course of choice
- SCM science course of choice

Track A: Help your student read aloud *Days Go By*, pages 77–80, "Where Will the Puppy Sleep?"

Track B: Have your student read aloud the Scripture passage in *A Child's Copybook Reader, Volume 2*, on page 54, then carefully copy the first phrase of the passage on page 55: "And when Jesus finished these sayings,". When he has finished the copywork, invite him to spell any word he remembers. Ask him to spell *Jesus*; if he is unsure, allow him to look at the word.

Math: Work on your selected math curriculum for 15–20 minutes.

Science: In your SCM science course, complete the first assignment for Week 23.

Lesson 114

Materials Needed
- *Delightful Reading, Level 3: From Words to Books* Kit (Track A)

- *Delightful Handwriting* teacher book (Track A)
- *Delightful Handwriting* student copybook (Track A)
- *A Child's Copybook Reader, Volume 2* (Track B)
- Math course of choice

Math: Work on your selected math curriculum for 15–20 minutes.

Track A: Spend 10–15 minutes working on *Delightful Reading, Level 3: From Words to Books.*
   Complete Lesson 69 in *Delightful Handwriting.*

Track B: Have your student carefully copy the next phrase of the passage in *A Child's Copybook Reader, Volume 2*, beginning on page 55: "the crowds were astonished at his teaching,". When he has finished the copywork, invite him to spell any word he remembers. Ask him to spell *were*; if he is unsure, allow him to look at the word. See if he can also spell *when*.

Lesson 115

Materials Needed
- *Delightful Reading, Level 3: From Words to Books* Kit (Track A)
- *Delightful Handwriting* teacher book (Track A)
- *Delightful Handwriting* student copybook (Track A)
- *More Busy Times* (Track B)
- Math course of choice
- SCM science course of choice

Track A: Spend 10–15 minutes working on *Delightful Reading, Level 3: From Words to Books.*
   Complete Lesson 70 in *Delightful Handwriting.*

Track B: Help your student read aloud *More Busy Times*, pages 51–64, "Another Special Day."

Math: Work on your selected math curriculum for 15–20 minutes.

Science: In your SCM science course, complete the second assignment for Week 23.

Lesson 116

Materials Needed
- *Delightful Handwriting* teacher book (Track A)
- *Delightful Handwriting* student copybook (Track A)
- *Days Go By* (Track A)
- *A Child's Copybook Reader, Volume 2* (Track B)
- Math course of choice
- (Optional) *Journaling a Year in Nature* notebooks

Math: Work on your selected math curriculum for 15–20 minutes.

Track A: Complete Lesson 71 in *Delightful Handwriting*.
    Help your student read aloud *Days Go By*, pages 81–84, "A Farm Dog."

Track B: Have your student carefully copy the rest of the Scripture passage in *A Child's Copybook Reader, Volume 2*, beginning on page 56. When he has finished the copywork, invite him to spell any word he remembers. Ask him to spell *for*; if he is unsure, allow him to look at the word.

Nature Study: Take the whole family outside for nature study.

Lesson 117

Materials Needed
- *Delightful Reading, Level 3: From Words to Books* Kit (Track A)
- *Delightful Handwriting* teacher book (Track A)
- *Delightful Handwriting* student copybook (Track A)
- *A Child's Copybook Reader, Volume 2* (Track B)
- Math course of choice

Track A: Spend 10–15 minutes working on *Delightful Reading, Level 3: From Words to Books*.
    Complete Lesson 72 in *Delightful Handwriting*.

Track B: Have your student read aloud the Scripture passage in *A Child's Copybook Reader, Volume 2*, on page 58. If desired, review 6–10 of these words and his selected words from previous copywork lessons: *then, who, rain, been, rock, words, will, came, fell, fall, Jesus, were, when, for*. If your student is unsure about a particular word's spelling, allow him to look at the word.

Math: Work on your selected math curriculum for 15–20 minutes.

Lesson 118

Materials Needed
- *Days Go By* (Track A)
- *A Child's Copybook Reader, Volume 2*, if needed (Track B)
- *More Busy Times* (Track B)
- Math course of choice
- SCM science course of choice

Track A: Help your student read aloud *Days Go By*, pages 85–91, "Levi and the Puppy."

Track B: Use today and tomorrow to catch up on any assigned reading and writing in *A Child's Copybook Reader, Volume 2*, as needed. If desired, review 6–10 of these words and his selected words from copywork lessons in Term 1: *and, all, things, them, each, that, made, their, in, at, God, the, running, sunset, up,* *winter, summer, garden, one, trees, we, water, day, see, tell, is, has, had, two, but, look, get, by, down, this, like.* If your student is unsure about a particular word's spelling, allow him to look at the word.

Help your student read aloud *More Busy Times*, pages 66–75, "The Wolf Story."

Math: Work on your selected math curriculum for 15–20 minutes.

Science: In your SCM science course, complete the first assignment for Week 24.

Lesson 119

Materials Needed
- *Delightful Reading, Level 3: From Words to Books* Kit (Track A)
- *Delightful Handwriting* teacher book (Track A)
- *Delightful Handwriting* student copybook (Track A)
- *A Child's Copybook Reader, Volume 2*, if needed (Track B)
- Math course of choice

Math: Work on your selected math curriculum for 15–20 minutes.

Track A: Spend 10–15 minutes working on *Delightful Reading, Level 3: From Words to Books*.
Complete Lesson 73 in *Delightful Handwriting*.

Track B: Use today to catch up on any assigned reading and writing in *A Child's Copybook Reader, Volume 2*, as needed. If desired, review 6–10 of these words and his selected words from copywork lessons in Term 2: *other, my, out, think, its, go, was, play, so, about, her, said, love, did, you, with, on, his, boys, they, are, cart, he, to, digs, pigs, last, do, much.* If your student is unsure about a particular word's spelling, allow him to look at the word.

Lesson 120

Materials Needed
- *Delightful Reading, Level 3: From Words to Books* Kit (Track A)
- *Delightful Handwriting* teacher book (Track A)
- *Delightful Handwriting* student copybook (Track A)
- *More Busy Times* (Track B)
- Math course of choice
- SCM science course of choice

Track A: Spend 10–15 minutes working on *Delightful Reading, Level 3: From Words to Books*.
Complete Lesson 74 in *Delightful Handwriting*.

Track B: Help your student read aloud *More Busy Times*, pages 76–86, "The Doll Story."

Notes

Math: Work on your selected math curriculum for 15–20 minutes.

Science: In your SCM science course, complete the second assignment for Week 24.

Term 3

(12 weeks; 5 lessons/week)

Term 3 Resources List

- Math course of choice
- Simply Charlotte Mason (SCM) science course of choice
- *Journaling a Year in Nature* notebooks (optional)

Track A

- *Delightful Reading, Level 3: From Words to Books* Kit
- *Delightful Handwriting* teacher book
- *Delightful Handwriting* student copybook
- *Days Go By*
- *More Days Go By*

Track B

- *A Child's Copybook Reader, Volume 3*
- *More Busy Times*

Weekly Schedule *(most weeks)*

	Day One	Day Two	Day Three	Day Four	Day Five
	Math (15–20 min.)	Math (15–20 min.)	Math (15–20 min.)	Math (15–20 min.)	Math (15–20 min.)
		Science (15–20 min.)		(Nature Study)	Science (15–20 min.)
Track A	Delightful Reading (10–15 min.); Delightful Handwriting (5 min.)	Days Go By (10–15 min.); Delightful Handwriting (5 min.)	Days Go By (10–15 min.)	Days Go By (10–15 min.); Delightful Handwriting (5 min.)	Delightful Reading (10–15 min.); Delightful Handwriting (5 min.)
Track B	Copybook Reader (5 min.); More Busy Times (10–15 min.)	Copybook Reader (5 min.)	Copybook Reader (5 min.)	Copybook Reader (5 min.)	More Busy Times (10–15 min.)

Lesson 121

Materials Needed
- *Delightful Reading, Level 3: From Words to Books* Kit (Track A)
- *Delightful Handwriting* teacher book (Track A)
- *Delightful Handwriting* student copybook (Track A)
- *A Child's Copybook Reader, Volume 3* (Track B)
- Math course of choice

Math: Work on your selected math curriculum for 15–20 minutes.

Track A: Spend 10–15 minutes working on *Delightful Reading, Level 3: From Words to Books*.
    Complete Lesson 75 in *Delightful Handwriting*.

Track B: Have your student read aloud the stanza in *A Child's Copybook Reader, Volume 3*, on page 4, then carefully copy the first two lines of that stanza on pages 5 and top of 6: "The wise may bring their learning, the rich may bring their wealth,". When he has finished the copywork, invite him to spell any word he remembers. Ask him to spell *bring*; if he is unsure, allow him to look at the word.

Lesson 122

Materials Needed
- *Delightful Handwriting* teacher book (Track A)
- *Delightful Handwriting* student copybook (Track A)
- *Days Go By* (Track A)
- *More Busy Times* (Track B)
- Math course of choice
- SCM science course of choice

Science: In your SCM science course, complete the first assignment for Week 25.

Math: Work on your selected math curriculum for 15–20 minutes.

Track A: Complete Lesson 76 in *Delightful Handwriting*.
    Help your student read aloud *Days Go By*, pages 92–98, "Guess My Animal."

Track B: Help your student read aloud *More Busy Times*, pages 87–99, "The Doll Story (part 2)."

Lesson 123

Materials Needed
- *Days Go By* (Track A)
- *A Child's Copybook Reader, Volume 3* (Track B)
- Math course of choice

Track A: Help your student read aloud *Days Go By*, pages 100–105, "Ducks, Ducks, Ducks!"

Track B: Have your student carefully copy the rest of the stanza in *A Child's Copybook Reader, Volume 3*, on pages 6 and 7. When he has finished the copywork, invite him to spell any word he remembers. Ask him to spell *some*; if he is unsure, allow him to look at the word. See if he can also spell *come*.

Math: Work on your selected math curriculum for 15–20 minutes.

Lesson 124

Materials Needed
- *Delightful Handwriting* teacher book (Track A)
- *Delightful Handwriting* student copybook (Track A)
- *Days Go By* (Track A)
- *More Busy Times*, if needed (Track B)
- Math course of choice
- (Optional) *Journaling a Year in Nature* notebooks

Math: Work on your selected math curriculum for 15–20 minutes.

Track A: Complete Lesson 77 in *Delightful Handwriting*.
   Help your student read aloud *Days Go By*, pages 106–111, "Rover."

Track B: Use today to catch up on any assigned reading in *More Busy Times*, as needed.

Nature Study: Take the whole family outside for nature study.

Lesson 125

Materials Needed
- *Delightful Reading, Level 3: From Words to Books* Kit (Track A)
- *Delightful Handwriting* teacher book (Track A)
- *Delightful Handwriting* student copybook (Track A)
- *A Child's Copybook Reader, Volume 3* (Track B)
- Math course of choice
- SCM science course of choice

Track A: Spend 10–15 minutes working on *Delightful Reading, Level 3: From Words to Books*.
   Complete Lesson 78 in *Delightful Handwriting*.

Track B: Have your student read aloud the stanza in *A Child's Copybook Reader, Volume 3*, on page 8, then carefully copy page 9. When he has finished the copywork, invite him to spell any word he remembers. Ask him to spell *would*; if he is unsure, allow him to look at the word. See if he can also spell *could*.

Math: Work on your selected math curriculum for 15–20 minutes.

Science: In your SCM science course, complete the second assignment for Week 25.

Lesson 126

Materials Needed
- *Delightful Reading, Level 3: From Words to Books* Kit (Track A)
- *Delightful Handwriting* teacher book (Track A)
- *Delightful Handwriting* student copybook (Track A)
- *A Child's Copybook Reader, Volume 3* (Track B)
- Math course of choice

Math: Work on your selected math curriculum for 15–20 minutes.

Track A: Spend 10–15 minutes working on *Delightful Reading, Level 3: From Words to Books*.
   Complete Lesson 79 in *Delightful Handwriting*.

Track B: Have your student carefully copy the rest of the stanza in *A Child's Copybook Reader, Volume 3*, on pages 10 and 11. When he has finished the copywork, invite him to spell any word he remembers. Ask him to spell *or*; if he is unsure, allow him to look at the word. See if he can also spell *no*.

Lesson 127

Materials Needed
- *Delightful Handwriting* teacher book (Track A)
- *Delightful Handwriting* student copybook (Track A)
- *Days Go By* (Track A)
- *More Busy Times* (Track B)
- Math course of choice
- SCM science course of choice

Science: In your SCM science course, complete the first assignment for Week 26.

Math: Work on your selected math curriculum for 15–20 minutes.

Track A: Complete Lesson 80 in *Delightful Handwriting*.
   Help your student read aloud *Days Go By*, pages 112–115, "Rover and Dad."

Track B: Help your student read aloud *More Busy Times*, pages 100–113, "The Grandmother Story."

Notes

Lesson 128

Materials Needed
- *Days Go By* (Track A)
- *A Child's Copybook Reader, Volume 3* (Track B)
- Math course of choice

Track A: Help your student read aloud *Days Go By*, pages 116–119, "Rover and Mother."

Track B: Have your student read aloud the stanza in *A Child's Copybook Reader, Volume 3*, on page 12, then carefully copy the first two lines of that stanza on pages 13 and top of 14: "We'll bring Him hearts that love Him; we'll bring Him thankful praise,". Point out the word *we'll* and its apostrophe. Explain that it stands for *we will*. When he has finished the copywork, invite him to spell any word he remembers. Ask him to spell *we'll*; if he is unsure, allow him to look at the word.

Math: Work on your selected math curriculum for 15–20 minutes.

Lesson 129

Materials Needed
- *Delightful Handwriting* teacher book (Track A)
- *Delightful Handwriting* student copybook (Track A)
- *Days Go By* (Track A)
- *More Busy Times* (Track B)
- Math course of choice
- (Optional) *Journaling a Year in Nature* notebooks

Math: Work on your selected math curriculum for 15–20 minutes.

Track A: Complete Lesson 81 in *Delightful Handwriting*.
   Help your student read aloud *Days Go By*, pages 120–124, "Rover and Rachel."

Track B: Help your student read aloud *More Busy Times*, pages 114–124, "The Finders-Keepers Story."

———————————————————————————————

Reminder: Get More Days Go By *for Track A for lesson 139.*

———————————————————————————————

Nature Study: Take the whole family outside for nature study.

Lesson 130

Materials Needed
- *Delightful Reading, Level 3: From Words to Books* Kit (Track A)

- *Delightful Handwriting* teacher book (Track A)
- *Delightful Handwriting* student copybook (Track A)
- *A Child's Copybook Reader, Volume 3* (Track B)
- Math course of choice
- SCM science course of choice

Track A: Spend 10–15 minutes working on *Delightful Reading, Level 3: From Words to Books*.
Complete Lesson 82 in *Delightful Handwriting*.

Track B: Have your student carefully copy the rest of the stanza in *A Child's Copybook Reader, Volume 3*, on pages 14 and 15. When he has finished the copywork, invite him to spell any word he remembers. Ask him to spell *ways*; if he is unsure, allow him to look at the word.

Math: Work on your selected math curriculum for 15–20 minutes.

Science: In your SCM science course, complete the second assignment for Week 26.

Lesson 131

Materials Needed
- *Delightful Reading, Level 3: From Words to Books* Kit (Track A)
- *Delightful Handwriting* teacher book (Track A)
- *Delightful Handwriting* student copybook (Track A)
- *A Child's Copybook Reader, Volume 3* (Track B)
- Math course of choice

Math: Work on your selected math curriculum for 15–20 minutes.

Track A: Spend 10–15 minutes working on *Delightful Reading, Level 3: From Words to Books*.
Complete Lesson 83 in *Delightful Handwriting*.

Track B: Have your student read aloud the stanza in *A Child's Copybook Reader, Volume 3*, on page 16, then carefully copy page 17. When he has finished the copywork, invite him to spell any word he remembers. Ask him to spell *be*; if he is unsure, allow him to look at the word.

Lesson 132

Materials Needed
- *Delightful Handwriting* teacher book (Track A)
- *Delightful Handwriting* student copybook (Track A)
- *Days Go By* (Track A)
- *More Busy Times* (Track B)
- Math course of choice
- SCM science course of choice

Science: In your SCM science course, complete the first assignment for Week 27.

Math: Work on your selected math curriculum for 15–20 minutes.

Track A: Complete Lesson 84 in *Delightful Handwriting*.
    Help your student read aloud *Days Go By*, pages 125–129, "Peter Comes Home."

Track B: Help your student read aloud *More Busy Times*, pages 126–136, "The Smallest Girl."

Lesson 133

Materials Needed
- *Days Go By* (Track A)
- *A Child's Copybook Reader, Volume 3* (Track B)
- Math course of choice

Track A: Help your student read aloud *Days Go By*, pages 130–133, "Rover and Peter."

Track B: Have your student carefully copy *A Child's Copybook Reader, Volume 3*, page 18. When he has finished the copywork, invite him to spell any word he remembers. Ask him to spell *may*; if he is unsure, allow him to look at the word.

Math: Work on your selected math curriculum for 15–20 minutes.

Lesson 134

Materials Needed
- *Delightful Handwriting* teacher book (Track A)
- *Delightful Handwriting* student copybook (Track A)
- *Days Go By* (Track A)
- *More Busy Times* (Track B)
- Math course of choice
- (Optional) *Journaling a Year in Nature* notebooks

Math: Work on your selected math curriculum for 15–20 minutes.

Track A: Complete Lesson 85 in *Delightful Handwriting*.
    Help your student read aloud *Days Go By*, pages 134–140, "Rover Learns."

Track B: Help your student read aloud *More Busy Times*, pages 137–148, "A Hard Day for Nancy."

Nature Study: Take the whole family outside for nature study.

Lesson 135

Materials Needed
- *Delightful Reading, Level 3: From Words to Books* Kit (Track A)
- *Delightful Handwriting* teacher book (Track A)
- *Delightful Handwriting* student copybook (Track A)
- *A Child's Copybook Reader, Volume 3* (Track B)
- Math course of choice
- SCM science course of choice

Track A: Spend 10–15 minutes working on *Delightful Reading, Level 3: From Words to Books*.
   Complete Lesson 86 in *Delightful Handwriting*.

Track B: Have your student read aloud the stanza in *A Child's Copybook Reader, Volume 3*, on page 19, then carefully copy page 20. When he has finished the copywork, invite him to spell any word he remembers. Ask him to spell *have*; if he is unsure, allow him to look at the word.

Math: Work on your selected math curriculum for 15–20 minutes.

Science: In your SCM science course, complete the second assignment for Week 27.

Lesson 136

Materials Needed
- *Delightful Reading, Level 3: From Words to Books* Kit (Track A)
- *Delightful Handwriting* teacher book (Track A)
- *Delightful Handwriting* student copybook (Track A)
- *A Child's Copybook Reader, Volume 3* (Track B)
- Math course of choice

Math: Work on your selected math curriculum for 15–20 minutes.

Track A: Spend 10–15 minutes working on *Delightful Reading, Level 3: From Words to Books*.
   Complete Lesson 87 in *Delightful Handwriting*.

Track B: Have your student carefully copy *A Child's Copybook Reader, Volume 3*, page 21. When he has finished the copywork, invite him to spell any word he remembers. Ask him to spell *him*; if he is unsure, allow him to look at the word.

Lesson 137

Materials Needed
- *Delightful Handwriting* teacher book (Track A)
- *Delightful Handwriting* student copybook (Track A)
- *Days Go By* (Track A)

- *More Busy Times*, if needed (Track B)
- Math course of choice
- SCM science course of choice

Science: In your SCM science course, complete the first assignment for Week 28.

Math: Work on your selected math curriculum for 15–20 minutes.

Track A: Complete Lesson 88 in *Delightful Handwriting*.
    Help your student read aloud *Days Go By*, pages 141–148, "Much More to Learn."

Track B: Use today to catch up on any assigned reading in *More Busy Times*, as needed.

Lesson 138

Materials Needed
- *Days Go By* (Track A)
- *A Child's Copybook Reader, Volume 3* (Track B)
- Math course of choice

Track A: Help your student read aloud *Days Go By*, pages 149–155, "Bess and Lady."

Track B: Have your student read aloud the stanza in *A Child's Copybook Reader, Volume 3*, on page 22, then carefully copy page 23. When he has finished the copywork, invite him to spell any word he remembers. Ask him to spell *these*; if he is unsure, allow him to look at the word.

Math: Work on your selected math curriculum for 15–20 minutes.

Lesson 139

Materials Needed
- *Delightful Handwriting* teacher book (Track A)
- *Delightful Handwriting* student copybook (Track A)
- *More Days Go By* (Track A)
- *More Busy Times* (Track B)
- Math course of choice
- (Optional) *Journaling a Year in Nature* notebooks

Math: Work on your selected math curriculum for 15–20 minutes.

Track A: Complete Lesson 89 in *Delightful Handwriting*.
    Help your student read aloud *More Days Go By*, pages 6–11, "Happy Birthday!"

Track B: Help your student read aloud *More Busy Times*, pages 149–156, "Nelson's Problem."

Nature Study: Take the whole family outside for nature study.

Lesson 140

Materials Needed
- *Delightful Reading, Level 3: From Words to Books* Kit (Track A)
- *Delightful Handwriting* teacher book (Track A)
- *Delightful Handwriting* student copybook (Track A)
- *A Child's Copybook Reader, Volume 3* (Track B)
- Math course of choice
- SCM science course of choice

Track A: Spend 10–15 minutes working on *Delightful Reading, Level 3: From Words to Books*.
　　Complete Lesson 90 in *Delightful Handwriting*.

Track B: Have your student carefully copy *A Child's Copybook Reader, Volume 3*, page 24. When he has finished the copywork, invite him to spell any word he remembers. Ask him to spell *than*; if he is unsure, allow him to look at the word. Discuss how it is different from *then* in both spelling and meaning.

Math: Work on your selected math curriculum for 15–20 minutes.

Science: In your SCM science course, complete the second assignment for Week 28.

Lesson 141

Materials Needed
- *Delightful Reading, Level 3: From Words to Books* Kit (Track A)
- *Delightful Handwriting* teacher book (Track A)
- *Delightful Handwriting* student copybook (Track A)
- *A Child's Copybook Reader, Volume 3* (Track B)
- Math course of choice

Math: Work on your selected math curriculum for 15–20 minutes.

Track A: Spend 10–15 minutes working on *Delightful Reading, Level 3: From Words to Books*.
　　Complete Lesson 91 in *Delightful Handwriting*.

Track B: Have your student read aloud the entire poem in *A Child's Copybook Reader, Volume 3*, on page 25. If desired, review 6–10 of these words and his selected words from previous copywork lessons: *bring, some, come, would, could, or, no, we'll, ways, be, may, have, him, these, than*. If your student is unsure about a particular word's spelling, allow him to look at the word.

Notes

Lesson 142

Materials Needed
- *Delightful Handwriting* teacher book (Track A)
- *Delightful Handwriting* student copybook (Track A)
- *More Days Go By* (Track A)
- *More Busy Times* (Track B)
- Math course of choice
- SCM science course of choice

Science: In your SCM science course, complete the first assignment for Week 29.

Math: Work on your selected math curriculum for 15–20 minutes.

Track A: Complete Lesson 92 in *Delightful Handwriting*.
  Help your student read aloud *More Days Go By*, pages 12–18, "Grandfather and Grandmother."

Track B: Help your student read aloud *More Busy Times*, pages 157–170, "Nelson and Dr. Wood."

Lesson 143

Materials Needed
- *More Days Go By* (Track A)
- *A Child's Copybook Reader, Volume 3* (Track B)
- Math course of choice

Track A: Help your student read aloud *More Days Go By*, pages 19–24, "Two More Surprises."

Track B: Have your student read aloud the paragraph in *A Child's Copybook Reader, Volume 3*, on page 27, then carefully copy its first sentence on pages 28 and 29. When he has finished the copywork, invite him to spell any word he remembers. Ask him to spell *if*; if he is unsure, allow him to look at the word. See if he can also spell *from*.

Tip: You may want to draw your student's attention to the period at the top of page 29 as the signal of the end of that sentence.

Math: Work on your selected math curriculum for 15–20 minutes.

Lesson 144

Materials Needed
- *Delightful Handwriting* teacher book (Track A)
- *Delightful Handwriting* student copybook (Track A)

- *More Days Go By* (Track A)
- *More Busy Times* (Track B)
- Math course of choice
- (Optional) *Journaling a Year in Nature* notebooks

Math: Work on your selected math curriculum for 15–20 minutes.

Track A: Complete Lesson 93 in *Delightful Handwriting*.

Help your student read aloud *More Days Go By*, pages 25–33, "At Grandfather's House."

Track B: Help your student read aloud *More Busy Times*, pages 172–182, "Peter's Bank."

Nature Study: Take the whole family outside for nature study.

Lesson 145

Materials Needed
- *Delightful Reading, Level 3: From Words to Books* Kit (Track A)
- *Delightful Handwriting* teacher book (Track A)
- *Delightful Handwriting* student copybook (Track A)
- *A Child's Copybook Reader, Volume 3* (Track B)
- Math course of choice
- SCM science course of choice

Track A: Spend 10–15 minutes working on *Delightful Reading, Level 3: From Words to Books*.

Complete Lesson 94 in *Delightful Handwriting*.

Track B: Have your student carefully copy the next sentence of the paragraph in *A Child's Copybook Reader, Volume 3*, pages 29 and 30: "The dog barks as a cart passes by, rumbling." When he has finished the copywork, invite him to spell any word he remembers. Ask him to spell *barks*; if he is unsure, allow him to look at the word.

Math: Work on your selected math curriculum for 15–20 minutes.

Science: In your SCM science course, complete the second assignment for Week 29.

Lesson 146

Materials Needed
- *Delightful Reading, Level 3: From Words to Books* Kit (Track A)
- *Delightful Handwriting* teacher book (Track A)
- *Delightful Handwriting* student copybook (Track A)
- *A Child's Copybook Reader, Volume 3* (Track B)
- Math course of choice

Notes

Math: Work on your selected math curriculum for 15–20 minutes.

Track A: Spend 10–15 minutes working on *Delightful Reading, Level 3: From Words to Books.*
     Complete Lesson 95 in *Delightful Handwriting.*

Track B: Have your student carefully copy the next sentence of the paragraph in *A Child's Copybook Reader, Volume 3*, page 30: "The carter whistles and cracks his whip." When he has finished the copywork, invite him to spell any word he remembers. Ask him to spell *whip*; if he is unsure, allow him to look at the word.

Lesson 147

Materials Needed
- *Delightful Handwriting* teacher book (Track A)
- *Delightful Handwriting* student copybook (Track A)
- *More Days Go By* (Track A)
- *More Busy Times* (Track B)
- Math course of choice
- SCM science course of choice

Science: In your SCM science course, complete the first assignment for Week 30.

Math: Work on your selected math curriculum for 15–20 minutes.

Track A: Complete Lesson 96 in *Delightful Handwriting.*
     Help your student read aloud *More Days Go By*, pages 34–39, "A Day with Grandmother."

Track B: Help your student read aloud *More Busy Times*, pages 183–191, "Peter Learns a Lesson."

Lesson 148

Materials Needed
- *More Days Go By* (Track A)
- *A Child's Copybook Reader, Volume 3* (Track B)
- Math course of choice

Track A: Help your student read aloud *More Days Go By*, pages 40–44, "Home Again."

Track B: Have your student carefully copy the last sentence of the paragraph in *A Child's Copybook Reader, Volume 3*, pages 30–32. When he has finished the copywork, invite him to spell any word he remembers. Ask him to spell *as*; if he is unsure, allow him to look at the word.

Math: Work on your selected math curriculum for 15–20 minutes.

Lesson 149

Materials Needed
- *Delightful Handwriting* teacher book (Track A)
- *Delightful Handwriting* student copybook (Track A)
- *More Days Go By* (Track A)
- *More Busy Times*, if needed (Track B)
- Math course of choice
- (Optional) *Journaling a Year in Nature* notebooks

Math: Work on your selected math curriculum for 15–20 minutes.

Track A: Complete Lesson 97 in *Delightful Handwriting*.
   Help your student read aloud *More Days Go By*, pages 46–51, "A Funny Animal."

Track B: Use today to catch up on any assigned reading in *More Busy Times*, as needed.

Nature Study: Take the whole family outside for nature study.

Lesson 150

Materials Needed
- *Delightful Reading, Level 3: From Words to Books* Kit (Track A)
- *Delightful Handwriting* teacher book (Track A)
- *Delightful Handwriting* student copybook (Track A)
- *A Child's Copybook Reader, Volume 3* (Track B)
- Math course of choice
- SCM science course of choice

Track A: Spend 10–15 minutes working on *Delightful Reading, Level 3: From Words to Books*.
   Complete Lesson 98 in *Delightful Handwriting*.

Track B: Have your student read aloud the paragraph in *A Child's Copybook Reader, Volume 3*, on page 33, then carefully copy its first two clauses on pages 34 and 35: "The wind whispers in the fir branches; the birds sing in them;". When he has finished the copywork, invite him to spell any word he remembers. Ask him to spell *birds*; if he is unsure, allow him to look at the word.

Math: Work on your selected math curriculum for 15–20 minutes.

Science: In your SCM science course, complete the second assignment for Week 30.

Lesson 151

Materials Needed
- *Delightful Reading, Level 3: From Words to Books* Kit (Track A)
- *Delightful Handwriting* teacher book (Track A)
- *Delightful Handwriting* student copybook (Track A)
- *A Child's Copybook Reader, Volume 3* (Track B)
- Math course of choice

Math: Work on your selected math curriculum for 15–20 minutes.

Track A: Spend 10–15 minutes working on *Delightful Reading, Level 3: From Words to Books*.
    Complete Lesson 99 in *Delightful Handwriting*.

Track B: Have your student carefully copy the rest of that sentence and the next in *A Child's Copybook Reader, Volume 3*, pages 35 and 36: "and the cat purrs, sitting under them. Dan chops up the logs." When he has finished the copywork, invite him to spell any word he remembers. Ask him to spell *under*; if he is unsure, allow him to look at the word.

Lesson 152

Materials Needed
- *Delightful Handwriting* teacher book (Track A)
- *Delightful Handwriting* student copybook (Track A)
- *More Days Go By* (Track A)
- *More Busy Times* (Track B)
- Math course of choice
- SCM science course of choice

Science: In your SCM science course, complete the first assignment for Week 31.

Math: Work on your selected math curriculum for 15–20 minutes.

Track A: Complete Lesson 100 in *Delightful Handwriting*.
    Help your student read aloud *More Days Go By*, pages 52–57, "Something to Laugh At."

Track B: Help your student read aloud *More Busy Times*, pages 192–200, "Peter Finds a Way."

Lesson 153

Materials Needed
- *More Days Go By* (Track A)
- *A Child's Copybook Reader, Volume 3* (Track B)
- Math course of choice

Track A: Help your student read aloud *More Days Go By*, pages 58–64, "Laughing at Levi."

Track B: Have your student carefully copy the last sentence of the paragraph in *A Child's Copybook Reader, Volume 3*, pages 36 and 37. When he has finished the copywork, invite him to spell any word he remembers. Ask him to spell *number*; if he is unsure, allow him to look at the word. See if he can also spell *of*.

Math: Work on your selected math curriculum for 15–20 minutes.

Lesson 154

Materials Needed
- *Delightful Handwriting* teacher book (Track A)
- *Delightful Handwriting* student copybook (Track A)
- *More Days Go By* (Track A)
- *More Busy Times* (Track B)
- Math course of choice
- (Optional) *Journaling a Year in Nature* notebooks

Math: Work on your selected math curriculum for 15–20 minutes.

Track A: Complete Lesson 101 in *Delightful Handwriting*.
   Help your student read aloud *More Days Go By*, pages 65–69, "Something for the Donkey."

Track B: Help your student read aloud *More Busy Times*, pages 201–211, "Trapping Mice."

Nature Study: Take the whole family outside for nature study.

Lesson 155

Materials Needed
- *Delightful Reading, Level 3: From Words to Books* Kit (Track A)
- *Delightful Handwriting* teacher book (Track A)
- *Delightful Handwriting* student copybook (Track A)
- *A Child's Copybook Reader, Volume 3* (Track B)
- Math course of choice
- SCM science course of choice

Track A: Spend 10–15 minutes working on *Delightful Reading, Level 3: From Words to Books*.
   Complete Lesson 102 in *Delightful Handwriting*.

Track B: Have your student read aloud the paragraph in *A Child's Copybook Reader, Volume 3*, on page 38, then carefully copy its first sentence on pages 39 and top of 40. When he has finished the copywork, invite him to spell any word he remembers. Ask him to spell *grass*; if he is unsure, allow him to look at the word.

Math: Work on your selected math curriculum for 15–20 minutes.

Science: In your SCM science course, complete the second assignment for Week 31.

Lesson 156

Materials Needed
- *Delightful Reading, Level 3: From Words to Books* Kit (Track A)
- *Delightful Handwriting* teacher book (Track A)
- *Delightful Handwriting* student copybook (Track A)
- *A Child's Copybook Reader, Volume 3* (Track B)
- Math course of choice

Math: Work on your selected math curriculum for 15–20 minutes.

Track A: Spend 10–15 minutes working on *Delightful Reading, Level 3: From Words to Books*.
    Complete Lesson 103 in *Delightful Handwriting*.

Track B: Have your student carefully copy the next sentence in *A Child's Copybook Reader, Volume 3*, on pages 40 and 41. When he has finished the copywork, invite him to spell any word he remembers. Ask him to spell *ducks*; if he is unsure, allow him to look at the word. See if he can also spell *fish*.

Lesson 157

Materials Needed
- *Delightful Handwriting* teacher book (Track A)
- *Delightful Handwriting* student copybook (Track A)
- *More Days Go By* (Track A)
- *More Busy Times* (Track B)
- Math course of choice
- SCM science course of choice

Science: In your SCM science course, complete the first assignment for Week 32.

Math: Work on your selected math curriculum for 15–20 minutes.

Track A: Complete Lesson 104 in *Delightful Handwriting*.
    Help your student read aloud *More Days Go By*, pages 70–76, "Mr. Brown and Shag."

Track B: Help your student read aloud *More Busy Times*, pages 212–226, "A Trap for Peter."

Notes

Lesson 158

Materials Needed
- *More Days Go By* (Track A)
- *A Child's Copybook Reader, Volume 3* (Track B)
- Math course of choice

Track A: Help your student read aloud *More Days Go By*, pages 77–82, "Levi's Surprise."

Track B: Have your student carefully copy the last sentence of the paragraph in *A Child's Copybook Reader, Volume 3*, on pages 41 and 42. When he has finished the copywork, invite him to spell any word he remembers. Ask him to spell *little*; if he is unsure, allow him to look at the word.

Math: Work on your selected math curriculum for 15–20 minutes.

Lesson 159

Materials Needed
- *Delightful Handwriting* teacher book (Track A)
- *Delightful Handwriting* student copybook (Track A)
- *More Days Go By* (Track A)
- *More Busy Times*, if needed (Track B)
- Math course of choice
- (Optional) *Journaling a Year in Nature* notebooks

Math: Work on your selected math curriculum for 15–20 minutes.

Track A: Complete Lesson 105 in *Delightful Handwriting*.
    Help your student read aloud *More Days Go By*, pages 83–88, "Peter Laughs at Himself."

Track B: Use today to catch up on any assigned reading in *More Busy Times*, as needed.

Nature Study: Take the whole family outside for nature study.

Lesson 160

Materials Needed
- *Delightful Reading, Level 3: From Words to Books* Kit (Track A)
- *Delightful Handwriting* teacher book (Track A)
- *Delightful Handwriting* student copybook (Track A)
- *A Child's Copybook Reader, Volume 3* (Track B)
- Math course of choice
- SCM science course of choice

87

Notes

Track A: Spend 10–15 minutes working on *Delightful Reading, Level 3: From Words to Books.*
Complete Lesson 106 in *Delightful Handwriting.*

Track B: Have your student read aloud the sentence in *A Child's Copybook Reader, Volume 3*, on page 43, then carefully copy it on pages 44 and 45. When he has finished the copywork, invite him to spell any word he remembers. Ask him to spell *into*; if he is unsure, allow him to look at the word.

Math: Work on your selected math curriculum for 15–20 minutes.

Science: In your SCM science course, complete the second assignment for Week 32.

Lesson 161

Materials Needed
- *Delightful Reading, Level 3: From Words to Books* Kit (Track A)
- *Delightful Handwriting* teacher book (Track A)
- *Delightful Handwriting* student copybook (Track A)
- *A Child's Copybook Reader, Volume 3* (Track B)
- Math course of choice

Math: Work on your selected math curriculum for 15–20 minutes.

Track A: Spend 10–15 minutes working on *Delightful Reading, Level 3: From Words to Books.*
Complete Lesson 107 in *Delightful Handwriting.*

Track B: Have your student read aloud the entire story in *A Child's Copybook Reader, Volume 3*, on page 46. If desired, review 6–10 of these words and his selected words from previous copywork lessons: *if, from, barks, birds, whip, as, under, number, of, grass, ducks, fish, little, into.* If your student is unsure about a particular word's spelling, allow him to look at the word.

Lesson 162

Materials Needed
- *Delightful Handwriting* teacher book (Track A)
- *Delightful Handwriting* student copybook (Track A)
- *More Days Go By* (Track A)
- *More Busy Times* (Track B)
- Math course of choice
- SCM science course of choice

Science: In your SCM science course, complete the first assignment for Week 33.

Math: Work on your selected math curriculum for 15–20 minutes.

Track A: Complete Lesson 108 in *Delightful Handwriting*.

Help your student read aloud *More Days Go By*, pages 90–95, "Winter Is Here!"

Track B: Help your student read aloud *More Busy Times*, pages 228–238, "Susan and her Friends."

Lesson 163

Materials Needed
- *More Days Go By* (Track A)
- *A Child's Copybook Reader, Volume 3* (Track B)
- Math course of choice

Track A: Help your student read aloud *More Days Go By*, pages 96–104, "The Snow Family."

Track B: Have your student read aloud the Scripture passage in *A Child's Copybook Reader, Volume 3*, on page 48, then carefully copy the first part of it on pages 49 and 50: "Consider the lilies, how they grow: they neither toil nor spin,". When he has finished the copywork, invite him to spell any word he remembers. Ask him to spell *how*; if he is unsure, allow him to look at the word. See if he can also spell *now*.

Math: Work on your selected math curriculum for 15–20 minutes.

Lesson 164

Materials Needed
- *Delightful Handwriting* teacher book (Track A)
- *Delightful Handwriting* student copybook (Track A)
- *More Days Go By* (Track A)
- *More Busy Times* (Track B)
- Math course of choice
- (Optional) *Journaling a Year in Nature* notebooks

Math: Work on your selected math curriculum for 15–20 minutes.

Track A: Complete Lesson 109 in *Delightful Handwriting*.

Help your student read aloud *More Days Go By*, pages 105–112, "Who Took the Corn?"

Track B: Help your student read aloud *More Busy Times*, pages 239–248, "A Friend for Susan."

Nature Study: Take the whole family outside for nature study.

Notes

Lesson 165

Materials Needed
- *Delightful Reading, Level 3: From Words to Books* Kit (Track A)
- *Delightful Handwriting* teacher book (Track A)
- *Delightful Handwriting* student copybook (Track A)
- *A Child's Copybook Reader, Volume 3* (Track B)
- Math course of choice
- SCM science course of choice

Track A: Spend 10–15 minutes working on *Delightful Reading, Level 3: From Words to Books*.
  Complete Lesson 110 in *Delightful Handwriting*.

Track B: Have your student carefully copy the rest of the sentence in *A Child's Copybook Reader, Volume 3*, on pages 50 and 51. When he has finished the copywork, invite him to spell any word he remembers. Ask him to spell *not*; if he is unsure, allow him to look at the word.

Math: Work on your selected math curriculum for 15–20 minutes.

Science: In your SCM science course, complete the second assignment for Week 33.

Lesson 166

Materials Needed
- *Delightful Reading, Level 3: From Words to Books* Kit (Track A)
- *Delightful Handwriting* teacher book (Track A)
- *Delightful Handwriting* student copybook (Track A)
- *A Child's Copybook Reader, Volume 3* (Track B)
- Math course of choice

Math: Work on your selected math curriculum for 15–20 minutes.

Track A: Spend 10–15 minutes working on *Delightful Reading, Level 3: From Words to Books*.
  Complete Lesson 111 in *Delightful Handwriting*.

Track B: Have your student carefully copy more of the Scripture passage in *A Child's Copybook Reader, Volume 3*, on pages 51 and 52: "But if God so clothes the grass, which is alive in the field today, and tomorrow is thrown into the oven,". When he has finished the copywork, invite him to spell any word he remembers. Ask him to spell *which*; if he is unsure, allow him to look at the word.

Lesson 167

Materials Needed
- *Delightful Handwriting* teacher book (Track A)
- *Delightful Handwriting* student copybook (Track A)
- *More Days Go By* (Track A)
- *More Busy Times* (Track B)
- Math course of choice
- SCM science course of choice

Science: In your SCM science course, complete the first assignment for Week 34.

Math: Work on your selected math curriculum for 15–20 minutes.

Track A: Complete Lesson 112 in *Delightful Handwriting*.
   Help your student read aloud *More Days Go By*, pages 113–117, "The Bird Feeder."

Track B: Help your student read aloud *More Busy Times*, pages 249–261, "Susan Tries."

Lesson 168

Materials Needed
- *More Days Go By* (Track A)
- *A Child's Copybook Reader, Volume 3* (Track B)
- Math course of choice

Track A: Help your student read aloud *More Days Go By*, pages 118–123, "The Funny Bird."

Track B: Have your student carefully copy the rest of the Scripture passage in *A Child's Copybook Reader, Volume 3*, on page 53. When he has finished the copywork, invite him to spell any word he remembers. Ask him to spell *more*; if he is unsure, allow him to look at the word.

Math: Work on your selected math curriculum for 15–20 minutes.

Lesson 169

Materials Needed
- *Delightful Handwriting* teacher book (Track A)
- *Delightful Handwriting* student copybook (Track A)
- *More Days Go By* (Track A)
- *More Busy Times* (Track B)
- Math course of choice
- (Optional) *Journaling a Year in Nature* notebooks

Math: Work on your selected math curriculum for 15–20 minutes.

Track A: Complete Lesson 113 in *Delightful Handwriting*.

Help your student read aloud *More Days Go By*, pages 124–129, "The Toy Farm."

Track B: Help your student read aloud *More Busy Times*, pages 262–272, "Levi's Extra Fun."

Nature Study: Take the whole family outside for nature study.

Lesson 170

Materials Needed
- *Delightful Reading, Level 3: From Words to Books* Kit (Track A)
- *Delightful Handwriting* teacher book (Track A)
- *Delightful Handwriting* student copybook (Track A)
- *A Child's Copybook Reader, Volume 3* (Track B)
- Math course of choice
- SCM science course of choice

Track A: Spend 10–15 minutes working on *Delightful Reading, Level 3: From Words to Books*.

Complete Lesson 114 in *Delightful Handwriting*.

Track B: Have your student read aloud the Scripture passage in *A Child's Copybook Reader, Volume 3*, on page 54.

Math: Work on your selected math curriculum for 15–20 minutes.

Science: In your SCM science course, complete the second assignment for Week 34.

Lesson 171

Materials Needed
- *Delightful Reading, Level 3: From Words to Books* Kit (Track A)
- *Delightful Handwriting* teacher book (Track A)
- *Delightful Handwriting* student copybook (Track A)
- *A Child's Copybook Reader, Volume 3* (Track B)
- Math course of choice

Math: Work on your selected math curriculum for 15–20 minutes.

Track A: Spend 10–15 minutes working on *Delightful Reading, Level 3: From Words to Books*.

Complete Lesson 115 in *Delightful Handwriting*.

Track B: Have your student carefully copy the first sentence of the Scripture passage in *A Child's Copybook Reader, Volume 3*, on pages 55 and top of 56. When he has finished the copywork, invite him to spell any word he remembers. Ask him to spell *what*; if he is unsure, allow him to look at the word.

Lesson 172

Materials Needed
- *Delightful Handwriting* teacher book (Track A)
- *Delightful Handwriting* student copybook (Track A)
- *More Days Go By* (Track A)
- *More Busy Times* (Track B)
- Math course of choice
- SCM science course of choice

Science: In your SCM science course, complete the first assignment for Week 35.

Math: Work on your selected math curriculum for 15–20 minutes.

Track A: Complete Lesson 116 in *Delightful Handwriting*.
   Help your student read aloud *More Days Go By*, pages 130–134, "The New Toy Barn."

Track B: Help your student read aloud *More Busy Times*, pages 273–285, "The Bobsled Bus."

Lesson 173

Materials Needed
- *More Days Go By* (Track A)
- *A Child's Copybook Reader, Volume 3* (Track B)
- Math course of choice

Track A: Help your student read aloud *More Days Go By*, pages 135–140, "Miriam and the Toy Barn."

Track B: Have your student carefully copy the next phrase of the Scripture passage in *A Child's Copybook Reader, Volume 3*, on pages 56 and 57: "For all the nations of the world seek after these things,". When he has finished the copywork, invite him to spell any word he remembers. Ask him to spell *after*; if he is unsure, allow him to look at the word.

Math: Work on your selected math curriculum for 15–20 minutes.

Lesson 174

Materials Needed
- *Delightful Handwriting* teacher book (Track A)

- *Delightful Handwriting* student copybook (Track A)
- *More Days Go By* (Track A)
- *More Busy Times*, if needed (Track B)
- Math course of choice
- (Optional) *Journaling a Year in Nature* notebooks

Math: Work on your selected math curriculum for 15–20 minutes.

Track A: Complete Lesson 117 in *Delightful Handwriting*.
    Help your student read aloud *More Days Go By*, pages 142–147, "Teacher Dan's Surprise."

Track B: Use today and next week to catch up on any assigned reading in *More Busy Times*, as needed.

Nature Study: Take the whole family outside for nature study.

Lesson 175

Materials Needed
- *Delightful Reading, Level 3: From Words to Books* Kit (Track A)
- *Delightful Handwriting* teacher book (Track A)
- *Delightful Handwriting* student copybook (Track A)
- *A Child's Copybook Reader, Volume 3* (Track B)
- Math course of choice
- SCM science course of choice

Track A: Spend 10–15 minutes working on *Delightful Reading, Level 3: From Words to Books*.
    Complete Lesson 118 in *Delightful Handwriting*.

Track B: Have your student carefully copy *A Child's Copybook Reader, Volume 3*, the rest of page 57. When he has finished the copywork, invite him to spell any word he remembers. Ask him to spell *your*; if he is unsure, allow him to look at the word.

Math: Work on your selected math curriculum for 15–20 minutes.

Science: In your SCM science course, complete the second assignment for Week 35.

Lesson 176

Materials Needed
- *Delightful Reading, Level 3: From Words to Books* Kit (Track A)
- *Delightful Handwriting* teacher book (Track A)
- *Delightful Handwriting* student copybook (Track A)
- *A Child's Copybook Reader, Volume 3* (Track B)
- Math course of choice

Math: Work on your selected math curriculum for 15–20 minutes.

Track A: Spend 10–15 minutes working on *Delightful Reading, Level 3: From Words to Books*.
  Complete Lesson 119 in *Delightful Handwriting*.

Track B: Have your student carefully copy *A Child's Copybook Reader, Volume 3*, page 58. When he has finished the copywork, invite him to spell any word he remembers. Ask him to spell *seek*; if he is unsure, allow him to look at the word.

Lesson 177

Materials Needed
  • *Delightful Handwriting* teacher book (Track A)
  • *Delightful Handwriting* student copybook (Track A)
  • *More Days Go By* (Track A)
  • *More Busy Times*, if needed (Track B)
  • Math course of choice
  • SCM science course of choice

Science: In your SCM science course, complete the first assignment for Week 36.

Math: Work on your selected math curriculum for 15–20 minutes.

Track A: Complete Lesson 120 in *Delightful Handwriting*.
  Help your student read aloud *More Days Go By*, pages 148–155, "An Exciting Day."

Track B: Use today to catch up on any assigned reading in *More Busy Times*, as needed.

Lesson 178

Materials Needed
  • *More Days Go By* (Track A)
  • *A Child's Copybook Reader, Volume 3* (Track B)
  • Math course of choice

Track A: Help your student read aloud *More Days Go By*, pages 156–162, "The Best Pet of All."

Track B: Have your student read aloud the Scripture passage in *A Child's Copybook Reader, Volume 3*, on page 59. If desired, review 6–10 of these words and his selected words from previous copywork lessons: *how, now, not, which, more, what, after, your, seek*. If your student is unsure about a particular word's spelling, allow him to look at the word.

Math: Work on your selected math curriculum for 15–20 minutes.

Lesson 179

Materials Needed
- *Delightful Handwriting* teacher book (Track A)
- *Delightful Handwriting* student copybook (Track A)
- *More Days Go By* (Track A)
- *More Busy Times*, if needed (Track B)
- Math course of choice
- (Optional) *Journaling a Year in Nature* notebooks

Math: Work on your selected math curriculum for 15–20 minutes.

Track A: Complete Lesson 121 in *Delightful Handwriting*.
    Help your student read aloud *More Days Go By*, pages 163–167, "Good-by, Grade One."

Track B: Use today to catch up on any assigned reading in *More Busy Times*, as needed.

Nature Study: Take the whole family outside for nature study.

Lesson 180

Materials Needed
- *Delightful Reading, Level 3: From Words to Books* Kit (Track A)
- *Delightful Handwriting* teacher book (Track A)
- *Delightful Handwriting* student copybook (Track A)
- *A Child's Copybook Reader, Volume 3* (Track B)
- Math course of choice
- SCM science course of choice

Track A: Spend 10–15 minutes working on *Delightful Reading, Level 3: From Words to Books*.
    Complete Lessons 122 and 123 in *Delightful Handwriting*.

Track B: Use today to catch up on any assigned reading and writing in *A Child's Copybook Reader, Volume 3*, as needed. If desired, review 6–10 of these words and his selected words from copywork lessons in Term 3: *bring, some, come, would, could, or, no, we'll, ways, be, may, have, him, these, than, if, from, barks, whip, as, birds, under, number, of, grass, ducks, fish, little, into*. If your student is unsure about a particular word's spelling, allow him to look at the word.

Math: Work on your selected math curriculum for 15–20 minutes.

Science: In your SCM science course, complete the second assignment for Week 36.